No doubt you've been bombarded with "expert" advice from your parents, professors, and countless advisors. It's time you got advice you can really use— from fellow students who've been where you're headed.

All **Students Helping Students™** guides are written and edited by top students and recent grads from colleges and universities across the U.S. You'll find no preachy or condescending advice here—just stuff to help you succeed in tackling your academic, social, and professional challenges.

Check out these other **Students Helping Students**™ titles at your local or college bookstore, and online at Amazon.com, BN.com, Borders.com, and other book retailers!

Each one is packed with practical and useful advice from people who really know what they're talking about—**fellow students who've been where you're headed!**

NAVIGATING YOUR
FRESHMAN YEAR

As if getting accepted wasn't hard enough, dealing with the ups and downs of your first year at college is a unique challenge you'll be glad you only have to face once. Pick up this guide and learn from the first-hand experiences of dozens of college students who've survived their freshman year and lived to help you get through it without losing your mind. *($8.95)*

LEAPING FROM PUBLIC HIGH
TO A TOP U.

You worked your butt off for years to do well in school and be accepted by a top university. Congratulations. But if you think that the toughest part is behind you, think again. Get advice from fellow students who've done what you're about to do. Pick up this guide to help you prepare for and tackle the academic, social, and personal challenges that you'll face as you make the transition from high school to a top university. *($6.95)*

GETTING THROUGH COLLEGE
WITHOUT GOING BROKE

Figuring out how to pay for college and get through it without thousands of dollars of unnecessary debt is one of the toughest things you'll ever do. As the costs of education keep rising, you have to be more resourceful, creative, and persistent in finding money to pay for it and learning how to manage the money that you've got. This guide is packed with practical advice from fellow students who've faced this challenge, made some mistakes, and can share their most valuable lessons with you. *($8.95)*

TACKLING YOUR FIRST
COLLEGE PAPER

Whether you wrote dozens of papers in high school or escaped without writing more than a few, acing your first few college papers will be a new and challenging experience. This guide will help you get ready, get organized, choose an interesting topic and a strong thesis, write a clear and error-free paper, and keep your sanity while you do it. *($6.95)*

FISHING FOR
A MAJOR

You might know exactly what you want to do with your life. Or you might have no idea at all. In either case, reading what other students think about finding a major that makes you happy can help you consider things you've not thought of. Find out how other students approach choosing classes, getting the best out of the advising system, thinking about a career and finding a passion—and you might discover more than just a college major. *($6.95)*

SCORING A
GREAT INTERNSHIP

Finding and getting a killer internship during college has no downside— you'll learn a ton, spice up your resume, meet new people, and hopefully get a few steps closer to knowing what you'd like to do with your life after college. This guide is packed with tips on how to find the best internships, get yourself noticed and accepted, and learn the most once you're there. *($6.95)*

FIND YOUR PASSION
IN COLLEGE

Part of what college is all about is helping us to figure out what we like to do and what we might like to do with our lives. To really do this, you have to go beyond academics, and explore your passions by getting involved outside of class. Think you might like to be a journalist? Become a reporter for your college paper and see what it's like. A life as a psychologist sounds like fun? You won't learn much about it in your psych class, but you might if you staff a counseling hotline. Pick up this book and use it to help you find your passion. *($8.95)*

To learn more about **Students Helping Students™** guides, read samples and student-written articles, share your own experiences with other students, suggest a topic or ask questions, visit us at **www.StudentsHelpingStudents.com**!

We're always looking for fresh minds and new ideas!

Students Helping Students™

CHOOSE THE RIGHT COLLEGE & GET ACCEPTED!

First Edition

NATAVI GUIDES

New York

Choose the Right College & Get Accepted!
First Edition.

Published by **NATAVI GUIDES**. For information on bulk purchases or custom promotional guides, please contact the publisher via email at sales@nataviguides.com or by phone at 1.866.425.4218. You can learn more about our promotional guides program on our website, www.nataviguides.com.

Cover design by Monica Baziuk.

Printed in the U.S.A.

Copyright © 2003 by NATAVI GUIDES.

ALL RIGHTS RESERVED.

No part of this publication may be reproduced, stored in a retrieval system, or transmitted in any form, or by any means: electronic, mechanical, photocopying, or recording.

ISBN 0-9719392-9-2

Library of Congress Cataloging-in-Publication Data

Choose the right college & get accepted!-- 1st ed.
   p. cm. -- (Students helping students)
Co-authors: Megan Hutchin, Siobhan Phinney, and Albert Suh.
   ISBN 0-9719392-9-2 (pbk.)
   1. College choice--United States--Handbooks, manuals, etc. 2.
Universities and colleges--United States--Admission. I. Title: Choose
the right college and get accepted!. II. Hutchin, Megan. III. Phinney,
Siobhan. IV. Suh, Albert. V. Natavi Guides (Firm) VI. Series.
   LB2350.5.C57 2003
   378.1'61'0973--dc21
                                                      2003010047

A NOTE FROM THE FOUNDERS OF
STUDENTS HELPING STUDENTS™:

Dear Reader,

Welcome to Students Helping Students™!

Before you dive head-first into reading this book, we wanted to take a moment to share with you where Students Helping Students™ came from and where we're headed.

It was only a few years ago that we graduated from college, having made enough mistakes to fill a *War and Peace*-sized novel, learned more and different things than we expected going in, and made some tough decisions—often without having enough advice to help us out. As we thought about our college experiences, we realized that some of the best and most practical advice we ever got came from our classmates and recent grads. It didn't take long for the light bulb to go off: We started a publishing company and launched the Students Helping Students™ series.

Our vision for Students Helping Students™ is simple: Allow high school and college students to learn from fellow students who can share brutally honest and practical advice based on their own experiences. We've designed our books to be brief and to the point—we've been there and know that students don't have a minute to waste. They are extremely practical, easy to read, and cheap, so they don't empty your wallet.

As with all firsts, we're bound to do some things wrong, and if you have reactions or ideas to share with us, we can't wait to hear them. Visit **www.StudentsHelpingStudents.com** to submit your comments online and find our contact information.

Thanks for giving us a shot. We hope that the student advice in this book will make your life better and easier.

Nataly and Avi
Founders of NATAVI GUIDES and Students Helping Students™

co-author

Siobhan Phinney graduated from Columbia University in 1999 with a major in English and a minor in Writing. Siobhan couldn't have been happier with her choice of college—she found one that was academically challenging and located in one of the most exciting cities in the world. Following graduation, Siobhan decided to make New York her home.

co-author

Megan Hutchin is currently a sophomore majoring in English and minoring in Italian at Middlebury College in Middlebury, Vermont. Tired of being cold all the time, she is now looking forward to a junior year abroad in someplace warmer, such as Florence.

co-author

Albert Suh graduated from Princeton University in 2002, with a Bachelor of Arts degree in Politics and a Certificate of Proficiency in Environmental Studies. While in college, he taught standardized test preparation classes to high school students.

Siobhan is the author and editor of the first part of this book about choosing the right college.

siobhan's note

Choosing the right college can be an overwhelming task. It will make a difference in your life and it's an important decision. What I learned from my own experience is that most of all, this is a very personal choice. It's definitely a good idea to get advice from people you trust, like your parents, friends, and counselors, but make sure that whatever you end up doing, it's because you want to and not because you're supposed to. A college that might make sense for your friends isn't necessarily a place where you'll be happy, so be honest with yourself and remember that this is your future you're figuring out.

- Siobhan

Albert and Megan are the co-authors and co-editors of the second part of this book about acing your college applications.

albert's note

As a high school senior, I was lucky enough to have the experiences of my older sister to guide me through the college application process. I remember looking through her old, dusty boxes, examining the differences between rough drafts and photocopied final copies and realizing the amount of effort necessary to come up with an application of which I could be proud. It's my hope that the advice in this book, based on my own experiences and that of many other students, will make your own college application process run a bit more smoothly.

Best wishes!

- Albert

megan's note

The best way that I found to stay calm during my own college application process was to keep some perspective on things. When you're finishing your tenth application and spouting off the list of potential schools to the two hundredth person who asks "So what are your plans for next year?" try to resist the urge to just give up. You're applying for the chance at an amazing academic and social opportunity. Be excited about it, and things will come easier!

- Megan

the contributors

The following college students and recent grads contributed their brutally honest advice, ideas, and personal experiences to this book. Thank you to all—this book couldn't have been written without your help.

Crystal Bodendorfer graduated from Emerson College in 2001.

Eben Burnham-Snyder graduated from the University of Wisconsin - Madison in 1999.

Ben Cohen-Leadholm graduated from Wesleyan University in 1999.

Owen Confliti was a Broadcast Journalism major at Emerson College.

Margo Dobbertin received her B.A. from Barnard College in 1996.

Greg Dolsky is in his second year at Tufts University and is double majoring in Philosophy and Political Science.

Candace Duby is graduating from Sandy High School in Oregon and will attend Oregon State University in the fall.

Colleen Egan majored in Acting and Tech Design at Adelphi University.

Annie Evans is a member of the class of 2005 at the University of Central Florida, where she is majoring in English Literature.

Mike Gallant is a senior at Columbia University, where he is majoring in Anthropology.

Greg Guenthner is a senior at George Mason University.

Arar Han is a senior at Boston College.

Amy Herzog received her B.A. in Theater from Yale University.

Gannon Hurley graduated from UCLA in 1998.

Elizabeth Hutchin is a senior at the University of St. Andrews in Scotland, pursuing a History degree.

Meredith James majored in Visual and Environmental Studies at Harvard University.

Janet Kang is a senior Psychology major at the University of Pennsylvania.

Sher Kung is in her second year at Brown University.

Lindsay Mann is a sophomore at Boston University, where he is majoring in Film.

Johanna Maron majored in English at Vassar College.

Kate McCulley is currently a student at Fairfield University, majoring in French and Sociology.

Patty McKeever majored in English Literature and Theater at Wheaton College.

Jen Miller graduated in 2002 from the University of Tampa with a major in English and a minor in Writing.

Elizabeth Monk is in her second year at Middlebury College in Vermont, where she is majoring in Psychology.

Caroline Moore graduated from New York University in 2001.

Ziad Naji is a student at Penn State University.

Meredith Neal graduated from Abilene Christian University in 2000.

Emily Newman is a junior Communications major at the University of Pennsylvania.

Cicely Ott is a sophomore Philosophy major at Middlebury College. She is also minoring in Studio Art.

Ara Parseghian is a freshman at Princeton University.

Josh Pasek is a sophomore at Pomona College.

Holly Ann Popowski is a senior at New York University, where she is a Philosophy major.

Emily Regas majored in Dance and Psychology at the University of California - Santa Barbara.

Lori Roberts majored in Psychology at Southwest Texas State University.

Rachel Roberts graduated from Oberlin College with a major in Theater.

Amy Rodgers received a B.A. in Literature/Writing from Columbia University.

Meg Ryan is a sophomore at Pomona College where she is a double major in Psychology and Government.

John Sawyer majored in Business and French at Millsaps College.

Rachel Skerritt graduated from the University of Pennsylvania in 1999 with a B.A. in English and an M.A. in Education.

Sara Steinberger is a sophomore double major in Classical Studies and Political Sciences at the University of Pennyslvania.

Michael Tilley graduated from Colgate University.

Tracy Toon received her B.A. from Columbia University.

Christi Tritton is a sophomore at Skidmore College and is majoring in Psychology.

Eric Vos is majoring in International Studies at Middlebury College, where he is currently in his second year.

Owen Whitehurst is a freshman at Emory University.

Anna Wiencrot is currently a student at Vassar College, majoring in Drama.

Christopher Wipf graduated from Dartmouth College.

Mike Yank graduated from Harvard University in 2002, where he majored in History and Science.

Christina Zaroulis is a freshman Government major at Harvard University.

Rebecca Ann Zeigler is a student at the University of St. Andrews, where she is a senior Middle Eastern Studies and International Relations major.

Aimee Zygmonski graduated from Emerson College in 1997.

Many other students also contributed to this book, including students from Butler University, Cornell University, Fordham University, Ohio University, Smith College, SUNY - Albany, and the University of Wisconsin - Oshkosh.

To make sure that we're not off the mark in our advice, we asked several college advisors and admissions officers to contribute their thoughts to this book. We thank them for their invaluable input.

Bruce Bailey is the Director of College Counseling at the Lakeside School in Seattle.

Grant Calder is a college counselor and History teacher at the Friends Central School in Pennsylvania.

Ken Gabard is the Assistant Dean in Academic Advising and Admissions for the College of Arts and Sciences at Cornell University.

Monica Inzer is the Dean of Admissions at Babson College.

William Kennedy is the Co-Principal and an English teacher at the Friends Central School in Pennsylvania.

Sheri Salmon is the Director of Admissions for Birmingham-Southern College.

Nick Sproull is an admissions counselor at Butler University.

Lee Stetson is the Dean of Admissions at the University of Pennsylvania.

Thomas Tritton is the President of Haverford College in Pennsylvania.

Susan Semonite Waters is the Director of College Guidance at the Ranney School in New Jersey.

Richard Weimer is the Assistant Dean of Liberal Arts and Sciences at Northwestern University.

contents

1

what this book is all about

Everyone's experience in choosing and applying to college is different, but there is one common characteristic: STRESS. Figuring out where to go to college, writing essays, surviving interviews, doing well on tests, getting strong recommendations, figuring out how to pay for the ever-growing education price tag, dealing with parents, counselors, and countless advisors...all of that adds up to a good amount of stress, anxiety, and most of all, hard work.

The reason we know this is because every single one of us who has contributed to this book has recently gone through the college admissions process and dealt with the pressure and stress that come with it. We wrote this book to share with you some tips and strategies based on our own experiences as well as those of dozens of college students and recent grads we interviewed.

This book is made up of two parts. The first part is about choosing where to apply to college. This is an important decision and you should give yourself enough time to think about it, do your research, and make sure that you're making decisions that feel right to you. Sometimes this is easier said than done. You may find that you have conflicting feelings as you try to sift through not only your own perceptions and ideas, but also the advice you get from well-meaning parents and numerous counselors. Try to be open to advice and suggestions, but remember, you're the one who must live with your decision.

Like all big decisions, choosing the right college is a process—you go through lots of small steps before finally arriving at your decision. Your priorities change and evolve as you go along, and every now and then you might be surprised to discover that something you thought was really important to you no longer is. At first, this might seem unsettling, but it's completely natural. It means that you're learning more about yourself and your college options, and that's exactly what this process is about.

The second part of this book is made up of our advice on how to succeed with every part of your college application process. One of the hardest things to do is to make a case for yourself as a great candidate using some pretty impersonal things like essays, application forms, and standardized tests. It's not good enough to be smart, ambitious, interesting, and passionate—you have to let the admission committee know and believe that you're all of those things. You can do it, but it takes effort and guts to be yourself and create yourself on paper. We've tried to give you some ideas and suggestions on how to do this.

Applying to college is a bit like juggling. You have all of these pieces in the air—tests, essays, interviews, campus visits, financial aid forms, recommendations, etc.—and you have to keep them all going at the same time. No single system of organization works for everyone, but we've tried to include a lot of advice on how to juggle successfully, without driving yourself crazy. This is a stressful time and the more organized you are, the better off you'll be.

Getting into a college of your choice is a big deal. It's an important step in your life and the prospect of it being so important makes it kind of scary. As you go through this process, try to do your best to maintain some perspective and believe in a good outcome. You can't guarantee it, but if you do your best you'll be closer to it than if you leave it to luck and good fortune.

② what it's not

We're not admissions officers and we don't claim to know any kind of insider secrets that will guarantee you admission to the school of your choice. (And if anyone else is claiming to guarantee you admission, think twice about trusting that person or book.) What we've included in this book is a different kind of insider advice—advice from those who've been on the inside of choosing and applying to college and learned what works and what doesn't in getting through this process successfully.

Choosing where to apply to college is not the only major life decision you're going to make. It might seem that way right now, but it's not—it's the first of many to come. Once you get to college, you'll have plenty more: which courses to take, what you want your major to be, who you want as friends, and in which extracurricular activities to get involved. After college, you'll have to decide on a career path to follow, where to live, who with, and all that good stuff. It's hard to have perspective as you're going through this process, but you should try.

The college application process is not all about luck, nor is it foolproof. You can do everything right and not get into the college that's your first choice, or you might get in but not have enough financial aid and scholarships to pay for it. You can't control everything, but you can do your best at every step. If you know that you did your best you'll feel much better with whatever outcome than if you realize that you could've done more or better or sooner.

③

get organized

Whether you can't wait to start applying to college or are overwhelmed by the prospect of doing it, getting organized before you start is essential. If you know what you have to do and when, and if you have a system for organizing the hundreds of pieces of information that will be thrown at you, you'll be in control of this often unruly animal called the college application process. And being in control has a positive impact not only on your mental sanity—which is important!—but brings you closer to getting the result you're after: finding a college that makes you happy and getting accepted!

START EARLY!
▼
CREATE A REALISTIC TIMELINE
▼
ORGANIZE YOUR MATERIALS
▼
MAKE YOURSELF A STRONG CANDIDATE

START EARLY!

If you take just one piece of advice from this book, let it be this: START EARLY! The more time you give yourself to research schools, think about your options, write essays, and search for scholarships, the better off you'll be. Many of us learned this lesson the hard way, so take our word for it and avoid last minute stress, anxiety, and worst of all, missing out on an opportunity because you waited too long.

> *"If I could've done one thing differently it would have been to get a start on the whole process earlier."*

**Freshman,
Butler University**

How early is early? You shouldn't go crazy with it, but start thinking about college during your sophomore year. Do a bit of research, take the PSATs, and give some thought to the type of college that might make sense for you. By the second semester of your junior year, your college selection and application process will be in full swing, so get there prepared and with your mind focused on the right goals.

In the next section we put together a timeline to help you organize the many tasks you have to complete as part of this process.

CREATE A REALISTIC TIMELINE

The college selection and application process is a long one and you'll feel more confident and relaxed if you break it down into smaller goals and plan when you need to get

---

each one done. Get a planner or a desk calendar and create a realistic timeline that gives you enough time and includes every important step, from studying for standardized tests to going on college visits. Having a visual picture of this timeline will be really helpful.

Start with some deadlines that are set in stone, like when applications are due for Early Decision/Early Action and regular admission. As you start to find out when other events like college fairs take place, you can add them to your timeline. Once you know these fixed deadlines, you can create your own personal deadlines around them, like when to start researching and visiting schools.

Make sure that you revisit your timeline often and make any required changes. You might, for example, decide to take an additional SAT II subject test midway through your senior year. You should always put any major step like that on your timeline and leave yourself time to prepare.

It's a good idea to get into the habit of setting a specific and achievable goal for each week, like finishing an essay or working on vocabulary for the SATs. That way, you're not overwhelmed and you have a feeling of accomplishment, which we've found is pretty important.

We've put together a general timeline to help you get started. It contains the main steps most of us go through as we choose and apply to college, but you should make sure to fit it to your particular needs and schedule. Here it is:

▶SOPHOMORE YEAR

- Start thinking about college. Check out a few college fairs in your area or at your school. Sign up for any college workshops that your school might offer.

- Meet with your guidance counselor to talk about your college plans. It's important to establish a relationship with your counselor—he or she can be extremely helpful in the college and financial aid application process.

- Talk with your parents about paying for college. It's important to have an understanding of how much you'll be expected to contribute and who will take the responsibility for filling out the numerous financial aid forms.

▶JUNIOR YEAR

Fall

- To get in the running for the National Merit Scholarship, take the PSAT/NMSQT. It's also good practice for the SAT I test. (You can also take the PLAN test. This prepares you for the ACT, which you may take later, and gets you thinking about your possible career interests.)

- Begin to prepare for the SAT or the ACT.

- Start to research scholarships.

- Think about which teachers, counselors, and employers you'll ask to write your recommendations and make sure that you're in touch with them.

- Start thinking about some of your initial college selection criteria.

Winter

- Continue to research potential colleges and start working on your "ideal college profile."

- Register for the SAT or the ACT and continue to study.

- Begin to take stock of your transcripts, activities, and jobs. If you seem to be light on extracurriculars, get involved in a few—it's not too late to bolster your arsenal.

- Begin to work on your scholarship essays and continue to research scholarships. (Make sure to write any scholarship application deadlines in your college application timeline.)

Spring

- Request information from colleges that interest you. Do further research on any that look interesting and start to get your initial list of possible schools together.

- Take the SAT or the ACT.

- Visit a few colleges during spring break. Just make sure that it's not spring break at the college—you want be there when the action is in full swing.

- Sign up for summer school if you need to fulfill any special requirements. Apply for a summer job or an internship and try to make it a great one. Or, consider going to study abroad for a few months—it's a great experience and can be awesome material for your college and scholarship essays.

Summer

- Visit more colleges.

- Request additional materials and applications from colleges where you're thinking of applying.

- Begin to work on your college and scholarship essays.

- Continue to apply for as many scholarships as possible.

- Consider taking a prep course for standardized tests.

September

- Schedule a formal appointment with your guidance counselor to talk about where you are in the college application process, your goals, and any questions. Talk about your preliminary college selections and get an opinion about how realistic they might be. Discuss financial aid and scholarships.

- Create a system to keep your application materials organized.

- Take the SAT or the ACT if you haven't yet, or if you want to improve your score.

- Continue to work on your college and scholarship essays.

- Request letters of recommendation from your teachers and counselors.

October

- Attend college fairs to find out more about the schools you're considering. This is a great opportunity to meet with admissions staff from numerous colleges all in one shot.

- Start working on your applications. If you're applying Early Decision or Early Action, start with those applications.

- Order transcripts for the colleges where you'll be applying.

- Visit more colleges if you need to.

November

- If you're applying Early Decision or Early Action, send in your applications.

- Request that your standardized test scores be sent to the schools where you're applying.

- If you haven't yet, take the SAT or the ACT.

December

- Continue to work on your applications and essays for regular admission.

- Begin to collect the required materials for the FAFSA, the main financial aid application.

January

- Make sure to check with your prospective colleges about any financial aid forms they might require besides the FAFSA.

- File the FAFSA as soon as possible after January 1st.

- Continue to apply for scholarships.

- Check with the teachers who wrote your recommendations to make sure they sent them in.

- Send in any finished college applications.

- Take the SAT, the ACT, or SAT II if you haven't yet, or if you need to improve your score.

February - April

- Review your Student Aid Report (SAR) and make any corrections, if necessary.

- Many scholarships have late deadlines, so continue to apply for any for which you qualify.

- As your acceptance letters start pouring in around mid-April, carefully consider your options. You should also be receiving financial aid awards—contact your school(s) and ask for more money if you don't receive enough aid.
- Visit or revisit more schools if you have to.

May

- By May 1st, you should have decided on a college and sent in your notification.

- Send your chosen college your tuition and dorm deposit, if required.

- Apply for any additional loans and scholarships, as needed.

Summer

- Work, travel, read, and relax! Enjoy this time and do something you're really happy doing. It's a good idea to take it easy, but we suggest that you read some good books to keep your brain cells working and ready for college.

ORGANIZE YOUR MATERIALS

"Trying to stay organized is a good way to alleviate some of the pressure. Knowing that you have a well-defined plan should give you a good amount of confidence."

**Recent Grad,
Princeton University**

You're going to be accumulating a lot of information during this process, so you need some way to organize it. If you don't have a filing cabinet, you can get an inexpensive box for files and some hanging folders, as well as some manila folders. Use a hanging folder for each of the colleges you're considering and make sure you have contact information for the important people at each school: dean of admissions, registrar, financial aid officer, etc. If you really start liking a particular school, you'll have a lot of information on it, so you can use the manila folders to sub-divide. Within each hanging folder, create sections like "catalog," "correspondence," "school newspaper," etc.

"I had a whole system worked out—where this goes and where that goes. I was very organized about the whole thing. You have to be. Sometimes there are four or five deadlines within a week of each other. It was an interesting juggling act."

**Sophomore,
Penn State University**

MAKE YOURSELF A STRONG CANDIDATE

As you begin your college search and application process, take stock of how you're doing in your classes, activities, relationships with your teachers, and so on. This is your opportunity to make yourself stronger as a candidate, so take advantage of it.

Here are a few suggestions:

- Make sure that you're taking challenging classes and doing as well as you can. If you need tutoring or help, get it instead of just letting it slide.

- Get involved in several extracurricular activities, but make sure that you're doing it because you're interested and passionate about the activity. It's much more valuable to have a few activities to which you're strongly committed than ten that you're doing just to make yourself look good. You'll be asked about your activities during college interviews and it's pretty easy to spot someone who is just doing something to look good versus someone who really cares.

- Think about which teachers and counselors you'll ask for recommendations and make sure that you put some effort into establishing a good relationship with them.

- If you don't read a lot, make it a habit to read a book a semester and a good newspaper, like *The New York Times*, at least several times a week. This is a great way to improve your vocabulary and know what's going on in the world.

Stressed about choosing the right college and getting in? You're not alone. Anyone who's been through this process knows how much stress and anxiety comes with it.

"What stresses me most about college is the decision. I want to apply to so many schools—I'm really undecided."

Senior,
Monticello High School

"Holidays with the relatives are the worst! You've just barely started senior year and everyone is already pressuring you about college. With family, the pressure is on even before you get going with your applications."

Senior,
Dunlap High School

"The application process really stressed me out and made me doubt myself: Did I volunteer enough? Are my grades high enough? Am I a well-rounded student?"

Senior,
South Lake High School

"What stressed me out the most is always feeling like I don't have enough time to get all of the required things done. The deadlines all seem to come so soon."

Senior,
Bangor Christian Schools

"Finding the college that's right for me was definitely the most stressful part of the whole application process."

Senior,
Manasha High School

This process is inherently stressful and you probably won't be able to avoid all of it, but here are a few tips to help you get through it as smoothly as possible:

- **Become a maniac for organization.** It sounds like an overused cliché, but if you're organized about what you have to do, when you have to do it, and what you need to do to get it done, you're half-way to success.

- **Trust your gut.** Advice from your parents. Suggestions from books. Your friends' opinions. The amount of information you absorb while choosing and applying to college is overwhelming and sometimes conflicting. Keep an open mind, listen to feedback, but remember to trust your own gut feelings and reactions to everything from where you should apply to what you write your essays about.

- **Be flexible.** Rarely do things turn out exactly as you planned, and if you're unprepared for change you'll be more stressed than if you expect some of it from the start. Your first choice school may turn out not to have a great major in a field that's caught your interest half-way through the application process and you might need to find another number one choice. Don't beat yourself up for being "wrong." Instead, give yourself credit for learning more about your interests.

- **Take breaks.** Day after day of college stuff can get overbearing. Give yourself a break once in a while, do something you really enjoy and that has nothing to do with college, and air out your mind. You'll feel better and work more effectively afterwards.

- **Know when to stop.** You should do your best on everything from researching schools to working on your essays, but there is such a thing as doing too much. If you're researching the 100th school or working on your 50th draft of revisions, stop and think about whether you're going too far and whether what you have isn't good enough already.

4

get to know yourself

There are so many colleges out there that the prospect of finding the one that's your perfect match can seem overwhelming. You may already know something about certain schools through things you've heard from friends, family, and reading college brochures, but how are you supposed to know which ones might be worth investigating and which one will ultimately be a good choice for you?

Think about it this way: You're trying to match two elements—yourself and a college. While it can be tempting to start looking at different schools right away, take some time to get to know yourself better. This involves taking stock of more concrete things like your academic standing, and thinking about the more intangible parts of you: your personality, your likes and dislikes, and what makes you comfortable or uncomfortable. If you begin your search with a solid understanding of yourself, it will be easier to figure out what you should look for in a college.

FIGURE OUT YOUR ACADEMIC PROFILE
▼
TAKE STOCK OF YOUR INTERESTS
▼
THINK ABOUT YOUR PERSONALITY
▼
BE BRUTALLY HONEST
▼
DON'T GO IT ALONE

FIGURE OUT YOUR ACADEMIC PROFILE

College is about more than just academics, but taking classes, doing well, and learning is a significant chunk of what you'll be doing. And you want to make sure that you go to a college that challenges you without being overwhelming. When the admissions officers read through your application, they'll also be thinking about this and will be trying to figure out how well you'll be matched up with the college's academic profile. Other criteria will be important as well—your involvement outside of class, your drive and ambition, and the diversity of your experience—but how well you do in school and on standardized tests are important considerations.

Try to be as honest as possible as you think about your academic profile. If your grades and standardized test scores aren't so great, that's okay, and there are many colleges where you can be accepted, learn a lot, and have a great time. But if you apply to schools that don't match your academic profile, you risk not having enough choices when it comes time to make your final decision.

Here are some questions you should consider. Their purpose is to get you thinking about where you stand academically and what college environment will be the best match for you:

- How difficult are your high school courses and how well have you done in them?

- What were your PSAT, SAT, or ACT scores? (You can always improve these, but think about how you compare generally to the other college applicants.)

- Are you taking any Advance Placement (AP) classes?

- How do you measure up to your peers? Are you one of the top students, near the top, or somewhere in the middle?

You should also think about your attitude towards studying and classes in general. Competitive colleges have extremely rigorous academics and if you don't like to spend many hours reading tough material, you might want to apply to some less rigorous schools.

- How curious are you about knowledge and learning in general?

- Do you have good study habits and an ability to discipline yourself and work independently? (It wouldn't hurt any of us to have better study habits, but think about how well you work on your own and how you handle difficult assignments.)

- How do you deal with pressure?

- Are you organized, good at managing your time, and prioritizing?

- Are you good at seeking help with schoolwork when you need it?

TAKE STOCK OF YOUR INTERESTS

You want to apply to colleges that offer great classes and majors in the areas that interest you. For example, if you can't go a day without statistics then you probably need to look at some schools with great statistics departments.

Think about the following:

- What academic subjects interest you?

- What types of things do you like to study?

- What are some of your favorite classes?

In addition to your academic interests, think about other things you enjoy doing—after all, you'll only be spending part of your time studying.

- What extracurricular activities are you involved in?

- Is it important for you to continue with any of them in college?

- What things do you like to do outside of school?

Try not to limit yourself too much. It's a good idea to choose a college that satisfies your current interests, but know that some of them will probably change. There are a lot of subjects and activities you haven't encountered yet and that may grab your attention once you get to college.

"Some people go into their freshman year convinced they are going to study one thing for the next four years, and then that's what they're going to do for the rest of their lives. Most people don't stick with that."

**Recent Grad,
UCLA**

BASKETBALL ISN'T EVERYTHING

by
Michael Tilley
Recent Grad, Colgate University

One of the most important variables for me during the college decision-making process was that I played a sport in high school and was adamant about doing so in college. I had my own list of criteria, which I insisted needed to be met, and which made finding the right school difficult. For example, I played basketball—difficult enough since I was a 5'8", 120-pound high school senior—and demanded that my choice be a Division I school. Not only was it to be a Division I school, but it had to be a good academic institution. Above all, I needed to play a significant role on the team; simply being a part of the group wasn't enough.

Ultimately, my college athletic career fulfilled my expectations, but I couldn't have been sure of how things would turn out. I now know that my success was largely the result of timing and circumstance. This awareness makes me feel foolish that I spent so much time agonizing over the details of so many college basketball programs because unlike choosing a school for its campus—a feature that is unchanging—nothing about college sports was ever guaranteed or predictable, nor could it have been. With a bit more maturity I might have saved my family and myself quite a lot of anxiety.

I sometimes also regret the emphasis I placed on basketball during the college selection process and the four years that followed. As I got older, I realized that sports are simply not that important, that many of my best college memories have nothing to do with being an athlete, that while I was privileged in some ways I missed out on many other opportunities, and that there are things much more significant than sports to be preoccupied with when choosing where to go to college.

THINK ABOUT YOUR PERSONALITY

Honest self-reflection about who you are and what you like is more likely to lead you to a school where you feel comfortable being yourself and supported in what you're trying to achieve. If you can find this, you'll feel happier in your surroundings and you'll be more likely to perform well academically. Party schools are only fun if you love to party, and conservative college environments will drive you nuts if you're more of an off-the-cuff kind of person.

Be honest about what you're like and don't feel like you have to be a certain way. Consider the following:

- How do you socialize—do you like small groups, one-on-one interactions, or large crowds?

- Do you like to be around people or do you need a lot of time to yourself?

- Are you the life of the party or more shy and reserved?

- Do you like to be close to your family or is being farther away healthier for you?

- Do you love big, bustling cities? Or do you start to suffocate unless you're being one with nature?

BE HONEST WITH YOURSELF

by
Jen Miller
Recent Grad, University of Tampa

When it came time for me to choose a college, I looked far and wide for where I would spend the next four years. All of my friends said they couldn't wait to move out of their house and start their real lives when they entered college, so I did the same. We turned up our noses at local colleges because we were too mature to be living that close to home. My final decision took me more than 1,000 miles away from the state where I'd lived my whole life.

After a month, I hated my new college. I was so terribly homesick that I almost transferred to the state school that my friends and I had scorned. While they enjoyed the distance, I floundered. I had been swept along in their priorities and forgot to examine my own. In their need to break from their families, I thought I'd need that, too, when in fact I didn't want to be so far away.

When I begged my parents to let me come home, they were firm that I should finish out the year at my far-away school. Eventually, the homesickness subsided and I learned to enjoy where I was, in part because I joined extracurricular organizations and met friends that became my college family. Transferring would've been costly, both money-wise and credit-wise, so sticking it out was the best decision. I still wish, though, that I'd considered the local school. It would've saved both my family and me a year of heartache.

BE BRUTALLY HONEST

The more honest you are in evaluating yourself, the more likely it is you'll find a college where you're comfortable. College is a great time to grow and evolve—there's no doubt about that. But try to be honest about your starting point: who you are and what's important to you now.

Most of us have no problem acknowledging our strengths. But, let's face it, it's not a lot of fun to sit down and think about those things that we just wish would go away. Do it anyway. Maybe you wish your grades were better, but if they're not, you'll need to apply to some less competitive schools to make sure you have all the bases covered. Maybe you wish you didn't get so freaked out when you're under pressure. But if that's the case, you're going to have to look for a college atmosphere that's more laid back.

It's also important to be honest about your interests and preferences and to distinguish them from those of your peers. What works for someone else might not work for you.

DON'T GO IT ALONE

You don't have to figure out everything on your own. Sometimes aspects of ourselves are so much a part of us that it can be difficult for us to see them. The people who know you well can help in your self-evaluation. Bounce some ideas off your friends, parents, and counselors. If there's something you're not quite sure about, ask them: "Where do you think I stand academically?" or "What type of campus setting might I strive in?"

Choosing where to go to college is a very personal decision, but it doesn't mean that you have to make it in isolation.

"*Those students who follow their noses usually find themselves at a school where they're successful and happy, and those who let others make the decision for them often end up at the wrong institution and pretty unhappy.*"

Assistant Dean of Liberal Arts and Sciences,
Northwestern University

5

figure out what you want in a college

After you spend some time thinking about your own likes and dislikes, you'll want to consider what it is that you want your ideal college to have. You might have heard your counselors talk about an ideal college profile—think of it as your college shopping list. You probably won't be able to find a college that has everything you want and you'll have to make some compromises. But having your preferences laid out will help you focus and save time. As you begin to research and visit schools, you can consult your ideal college profile and see how the various schools measure up.

KNOW YOUR ACADEMIC REQUIREMENTS
▼
CONSIDER ADMISSION DIFFICULTY
▼
THINK ABOUT SPECIAL PROGRAMS AND OFFERINGS
▼
DON'T FORGET EXTRACURRICULARS
▼
CONSIDER THE COST
▼
THINK ABOUT SIZE
▼
DON'T IGNORE LOCATION
▼
FIGURE OUT A COMFORTABLE SOCIAL TONE
▼
THINK ABOUT A PARTICULAR ORIENTATION
▼
WEIGH UP CO-ED OR SINGLE SEX
▼
CREATE YOUR IDEAL COLLEGE PROFILE

WE TALK WITH...

Anna Wiencrot
Junior, Vassar College

What sorts of things were important to you as you started researching schools, and did this change later on?

I thought I wanted to be a vocal performance major, so I looked at big schools with that as a major program. I wanted a big school because my high school was 4,000 people and I felt like I wanted something bigger. I visited Vassar because my grandmother went there, and I just totally fell in love with it. All the people felt right. So I researched that school and now that I'm here, I'm really glad I went somewhere small. My teachers didn't even know me in high school and here I'm really close to some of my professors. I know people on campus and don't feel like I'm just one little number.

Did you have an idea for a major and did you stick with it?

I sang all through high school and I felt that coming into college I had to decide what I wanted to do right away. So I thought I'd major in vocal performance. People had told me I'd change my mind, but I thought I wouldn't.

I'm so glad that I did. I think it's good to follow your interests in college, but you can always change half-way through. I'm now a drama and costume design major. I'd always done theater when I was younger and in high school. When I came here I thought maybe I should stop doing theater entirely, at least for a little bit, to see if it was really the right thing for me. Second semester I realized that I really missed it, so I took my first drama class and declared my theater major three weeks later. It was like letting a boyfriend go and then realizing it was really meant to be.

KNOW YOUR ACADEMIC REQUIREMENTS

Based on your interests, what courses and majors do you want your college to have? If you love theater you'll definitely want to apply to colleges that offer a theater major and have a strong theater department. But remember that your interests might change and evolve, and your college needs to have enough majors and departments that interest you so that you can switch without having to transfer.

> *"Keep an open mind about the fact that your interests change fairly quickly at college. Those words were said to me more than a handful of times but I ignored them because I thought I knew everything. After four years I realized that I'd changed dramatically."*
>
> **Recent Grad,**
> **UCLA**

In addition to the types of courses you want to take, you should also consider how you want them to be taught. Think about how you learn best, how much individual attention and guidance you need, and how disciplined you are about studying. Some college classes are taught as lectures: They have a large number of students and the professor lectures while you listen and take notes. You're responsible for keeping up with the reading, and there is usually not a lot of interaction with the professor or with other students during class. Many introductory courses are taught in a lecture format.

Smaller, seminar-style classes have fewer students. In these classes, there is more interaction with the professor and more opportunity for you to contribute to discussions.

You'll probably take some of each type of class while in college, but if you prefer smaller classes you'll need to apply to schools that offer a lot of them.

"For me, being in a lecture class with 300 other students wasn't a good match. I really like discussions and wanted more interaction with the instructor and other students in the class."

**Recent Grad,
Columbia University**

Another thing to think about is whether you want to attend a school with a structured curriculum, or if you're a more independent spirit who needs freedom to design your own program. Most colleges have certain courses that you must take, usually called the core curriculum, but the requirements vary from school to school.

Another important academic aspect to consider is this intangible but ever-present thing called academic tone— how much of an emphasis is placed on academics, how challenging the course work is, and how much is expected of you as a student. If you're the type of person who loves talking about ideas, studying, reading tons of dense material, and learning new things all the time, then you'll probably feel right at home in a college with a strong academic bent. If you were to attend a college where you weren't sufficiently challenged, you might end up feeling bored or uninspired. However, if you're the type of person who is more interested in things outside of academics, say sports or other extracurriculars, you might feel out of place in an academically competitive atmosphere.

"When students want to confine their college selection to such things as majors I always discourage it. You haven't had any college classroom experience, so keep an open mind. Go to college with a willingness to explore, to react, and to identify your own strengths and weaknesses. Don't commit yourself at this point."

Assistant Dean of Liberal Arts and Sciences,
Northwestern University

CONSIDER ADMISSION DIFFICULTY

There are a lot of people competing for admission at college and you want to apply where you have a chance of getting in. It's okay to have a couple of long shots, and later we'll talk about applying to a few "reach" schools, but they shouldn't all be.

We also don't suggest that you apply only to schools that are super-easy for you to get into. You're going to spend a few years and a bunch of money on your education and you want a school that will stretch you and allow you to grow intellectually.

> *"I got in everywhere I applied, but I shied away from applying to places I had little chance of getting into."*

> **Recent Grad,**
> **UCLA**

GOING BEYOND MY COMFORT ZONE

by
Rachel Roberts
Recent Grad, Oberlin College

When I visited Oberlin I knew I'd love life as a student there, but I was reticent about actually getting in. The students walked from class to class with confidence and wore clothes that showed their individual styles. Political perspectives were also displayed proudly—scattered signs and pamphlets dotted the academic buildings, highlighting the varied degrees of left-wing activism on campus. I looked forward to understanding it all.

The only problem was that I enjoyed the urban lifestyle that my hometown of New York offered me, and Ohio was a world away. I was also doubtful about my seriousness as a student. After attending a Women's Studies 101 course as a prospective student, I became convinced that all of the students at Oberlin were much more sophisticated than I was. I wasn't ready to enter an environment that might overwhelm me.

But after I was rejected from another school I applied to, I decided, despite my reasons for hesitating, to give Oberlin a try. Looking back, I'm lucky that the combination of nineteen-year-old low self-esteem and New York snobbery didn't keep me from the tremendous formative experience that I had while attending Oberlin. I met some of the best friends I've ever had, and I learned that I was capable of succeeding as a student, despite the academic challenges that confronted me. I graduated from Oberlin with a better sense of self and with a grasp of subjects I never thought I'd encounter.

THINK ABOUT SPECIAL PROGRAMS AND OFFERINGS

There may be special programs or offerings that you're looking for your school to have. Some of these may be necessities and others may be things that would be nice to have but you could live without.

For example, if you have any disabilities, finding a college that can accommodate them is a big priority. If you anticipate needing tutoring with a particular subject, make sure that this is an option at the schools you're considering.

Other things, like whether your college has a formal internship program or a great selection of study abroad opportunities, might be good options to have, but these aren't things that will make or break your decision.

"I wanted to start learning a new foreign language at college and Wesleyan had this great study abroad program in Japan. It intrigued me, and I ended up going to Japan during the first semester of my junior year at Wes."

**Recent Grad,
Wesleyan University**

WE TALK WITH...

Colleen Egan
Recent Grad, Adelphi University

What were the most important considerations for you as you began your college search?

I'm dyslexic and I have ADD, so I had strict criteria. If you're learning disabled it's important to know where your weakness is. I wasn't shy about it in my interviews, either. I said, "I'm dyslexic. What do you have to help me?" It's hard to say, but you have to say it.

Given your learning disability, what concerned you going into college?

For years I had a tutor and one of the things I was concerned with was that at the college level your papers go from two pages to ten. One of the problems I have is that I'll write something and it will usually take me a couple of days to find all the mistakes, so I need someone else to proofread it. I needed to know that there were tutoring services available to me. A lot of schools offer tutoring services, but it's just for the general public and it's usually students or graduate students. I was looking for a school that actually had a program for learning disabled students.

Were you able to find many schools that offered what you needed?

A lot of schools said, "Oh yeah, we can work with it," but the school I went to actually had a really good program. I had a dedicated tutor with whom I met twice a week and who really helped me out.

DON'T FORGET EXTRACURRICULARS

Extracurricular activities can really enhance your college experience and they're a great way to meet people with similar interests. This won't be news to you if you've already sampled some in high school. Maybe you've been involved in the drama club, choir, or a particular sport. You may like it so much that you just can't imagine living without it in college. If that's the case, you may be tempted when you're looking at colleges to stick to what you know and love, but keep in mind that there will also be lots of new activities to try out. Look for what's important to you, but be ready to discover new interests.

Siobhan's corner
▼

I've always been a busy type of person, so I was sure once I got to school I'd get involved in all kinds of activities. My first year, I focused on getting adjusted to my new environment and getting good grades, but in my second year, I found myself suddenly wanting to do everything. I started taking creative writing classes, and found that I liked playwriting best of all. So I joined the Columbia Dramatists, a club where everyone worked together to stage each other's work. Seeing scenes I'd written staged really helped me in my writing. And it was very rewarding to present them to an audience and see a response.
▲

"*Students' interests tend to change a lot, especially in the first and second years. Find out if a particular school offers a range that would make those changes possible without having to transfer to another college.*"

Assistant Dean in Academic Advising and Admissions for the College of Arts and Sciences, Cornell University

NOT EXACTLY WHAT I EXPECTED

by
Crystal Bodendorfer
Recent Grad, Emerson College

I've always been interested in music and radio. I wanted to go to college and later work in this field, so I chose to study broadcasting at Emerson College in Boston.

Emerson has had an operational radio station for over fifty years, and it broadcasts twenty hours a day. I hoped to get a slot on air, and with some hard work I was able to. I gained the vocational experience that I was hoping to get, working with state-of-the-art programming and broadcast equipment.

Emerson also boasted a wide range of production classes in which I'd hoped to partake. If I'd known that the popularity of these courses would mean that many students like me were not going to be able to study them, then I might've considered another college.

I moved from the Midwest to Boston to attend what I thought was the best college for communications in the U.S. It was important for me to make the most of my education. Although I didn't get all that I wanted, I was able to compensate for these things through my involvement with outside music production projects. Much of what I wanted to learn in college I actually ended up learning outside of it.

CONSIDER THE COST

"My biggest concern during my college search was finances. I decided to stay in Texas because of the in-state tuition. If it wasn't for financial reasons and wanting to stay in Texas to be near family, I probably would've been applying to many schools outside of Texas."

Recent Grad,
Southwest Texas State University

Any time you go shopping, you need to know how much you have to spend. The same holds true when shopping for a college. Never ever rule out a school just because it's expensive—each year more than one billion dollars is given out in scholarships, and there are many types of financial aid for which you and your family can qualify. But if your resources are limited, as they are for most of us, you want to make sure to apply to some schools that are not as expensive, just in case.

Talk to your parents about paying for college. How much will they contribute? How much will you have to pitch in? It's important to have this conversation as early in the process as possible so you know what to expect, look for a variety of schools in terms of cost, and apply for financial aid and enough scholarships to cover the bill. We go into much more detail on financial aid in a later chapter, but consider this component as you figure out what you need from a school.

THINK ABOUT SIZE

Colleges come in all sizes, from student bodies of less than 1,000 to those of more than 60,000. The size of your school does affect your experience, both academically and socially. There are pros and cons to both small and large colleges, and it's just a matter of deciding what's right for you.

▶SMALL COLLEGES

At small colleges, as in small towns, you're more likely to bump into people you know. This can be nice, but it can also be a bit annoying after a while.

Classes tend to be smaller, which means there is more of an opportunity to participate in discussions and interact with the professors. Professors are more likely to remember you, and because they know you well, they'll be able to write you informed references for jobs or grad school.

"My school was smaller and there was no graduate program, so I was able to work a lot more in my field of costume design. There just weren't that many people doing it."

**Recent Grad,
Abilene Christian University**

Sometimes people assume that small schools aren't all that diverse, but this isn't always true. Many small colleges attract students of all types of social, religious, racial, and economic backgrounds. Don't make any judgments until you do some research.

▶LARGE COLLEGES

Large colleges usually provide a wider range of course offerings. If you're undecided about the subjects you want to take, they give you the chance to explore many different fields. They also tend to have more lecture classes than small, seminar-style classes.

Not knowing half the people in your class is not too rare at larger schools—and it's not always a bad thing. If having a degree of anonymity is more desirable to you than having everyone know you, a large campus may be a way to go.

FINDING THE RIGHT PATH

by
Caroline Moore
Recent Grad, New York University

At seventeen, I aimlessly applied to college. I thought I wanted to in acting, but figured I should keep my options open. Some people suggested a small, elite liberal arts college, others a large state school where I would get the most bang for the buck. I chose the latter, a huge university twenty minutes from home.

After a semester of big parties, anonymous lecture classes, and very limited theater, I was done with my large state school. I didn't want to be just a number in the university system and I wanted to move away and live in a big city. I'd also decided on an acting major and needed to be in a better program. College could be my chance to move away and do something different, as well as an institution I could use to launch my career.

I searched for a new school, this time with a clear idea of what I was looking for. I wanted an urban campus on the East Coast, small classes, and a strong arts program. I ended up transferring to NYU. My experience turned out for the best, and I don't think that making the wrong choice at first was necessarily a bad thing. At the very least, I feel like I got to go to college twice. I probably would've wandered no matter where I went first. I was someone who needed to wander before the correct path became clear.

DON'T IGNORE LOCATION

"I wanted to go somewhere that was far enough away from home that I'd meet totally different people but was close enough to go home at least a couple of times a year."

Recent Grad,
Columbia University

There are a few things to consider with regard to location. One is your proximity to home. If you've never been away from home for an extended period, think about how you might feel once you're away. If it's important for you to be near your family, you should think about how close you want to be—a couple of hours or a couple of states away? Try to gauge how frequently you might want to visit, and if you're thinking about moving far away, take into account the expenses involved in traveling home.

"I knew that I wanted to move to the West Coast, so I chose three different schools in California. I wanted a change of lifestyle, a change of scenery, and to move away from home, to get out."

Recent Grad,
UCLA

If being near home is not a concern for you, think about possible regions in the country where you might like to live. Perhaps there is a particular area that has always interested you. College can be a great time to try out a new environment.

"If you're going to go to college, try to go somewhere that is as far away from what you're used to as possible, somewhere where you can test out your theories on life. What's the point in testing them out in surroundings you're already used to, that you've already mastered?"

**Recent Grad,
UCLA**

Setting is another really important consideration. Colleges are located in cities, small towns, the suburbs, and rural areas. Consider the setting in which you currently live and decide if you want to seek out a similar situation or try something new. All settings have their advantages and disadvantages—it just depends what you're looking for. On the next page are some of the pros and cons of the most common college settings.

Siobhan's corner

▼

As you figure out what you want, sometimes a great way to start is to figure out what you don't want. I knew that going to college in the boonies was not for me. I like the country just fine, but I also like to be where the action is. Being in a college town was equally unappealing to me. I just didn't like the idea of being around nothing but college students. I like diversity: being around different kinds of people and people of different ages. Going to school in a city was perfect. I like museums, theater, and going out to hear music. ▲

URBAN COLLEGE

PROS	CONS
Lots going on Diverse population Many places to hang out Tons of cultural activities Ability to have a life outside of school	Noisy Crowded Expensive Distracting Can be lonely

RURAL COLLEGE

PROS	CONS
Peaceful Lots of nature Lots of space Not as expensive socially Few distractions Intimate, small-town feel	Sometimes lonely and isolated Boring Not much to do Dependence on social life at school

"COLLEGE TOWN" COLLEGE

PROS	CONS
Caters to students Many cool places to hang out Friendly atmosphere Heavily populated by students	Not enough "regular" people Can be rowdy Tons of distractions Not a "real world" environment

"I always recommend that students seriously consider going to a college in a different part of the country than where they currently live. College is a great way to live in a different place without the obligations of family or a job that ties you to it. It's a great way to broaden your cultural horizons, sample a different way of life, different attitudes, and even a different climate."

Assistant Dean in Academic Advising and Admissions for the College of Arts and Sciences, Cornell University

FIGURE OUT A COMFORTABLE SOCIAL TONE

We've all been to a party where we felt really out of place or in situations where we just didn't fit in. It stinks. The last thing you want is for this to happen when you go to college. You want to feel comfortable being yourself and being around people to whom you can relate. That's why it's important to give some thought to social tone and figure out what would make you comfortable.

You can start off by thinking about your current situation. What kinds of people do you like to hang out with and what kinds of things do you do together? You don't have to seek a similar environment in college—in fact, it's probably a bad idea to limit yourself to what you already know really well. But know the general type of a social atmosphere you're looking for.

> "I think what was really important for me was to have a really diverse school, not just racially, but in terms of the kind of people who go there. At Harvard you get all kinds of people."
>
> **Junior,
> Harvard University**

The social tone of a school depends on the backgrounds of the students there and the types of things that interest them, including what they're studying. At some schools a certain political bent will dominate. The Greek system of fraternities and sororities can play a big role in campus life, or it may be entirely absent. Depending on the college, students can also be socially aware, artsy, dress conscious, career-oriented, studious, athletic, sophisticated, laid back, open, ambitious, fun, etc.. Think about the types of people with whom you want to spend the next four years.

We keep repeating this fact, but make sure that you're choosing something because that's what you want. It's all too easy to get caught up in someone else's idea of what's cool. Maybe your best friend talks all the time about the great social opportunities to be had at really big schools. But just because that's what he's interested in, doesn't mean it's good for you. Another friend might be dead-set on joining a fraternity or sorority. That doesn't mean that you have to. This is your life, so make your own choices.

THINK ABOUT A PARTICULAR ORIENTATION

If mixing with others from your ethnic background or faith is important to you, you may want to make sure that you have the opportunity to do so at college. Think about how much of a priority this is for you.

> *"I've been raised in a certain denomination and even though I wanted to go away from home to school, I wanted to feel like I was in a safe environment, one that was well-supported. I was sixteen hours away from my parents—it was important for me to be comfortable where I was."*
>
> **Recent Grad,**
> **Abilene Christian University**

Students from non-white backgrounds sometimes say they feel isolated on a predominantly white campus. If attending college with culturally (or racially) similar peers is important to you, find out about the student populations at the schools you're considering and look for those with diverse student bodies.

Some students choose to attend schools composed almost entirely of people from their ethnic background. Students at these schools often speak of a great feeling of camaraderie, as well as the benefits of having role models from their own culture. This might be a choice you need to consider depending on your own preferences.

WEIGH UP CO-ED OR SINGLE SEX

"At Vassar there is a strong female voice because it was one of the Seven Sister schools. I really liked that part of it, but I also liked the fact that it was co-ed."

**Recent Grad,
Vassar College**

While all-male schools are on the decline, all-female colleges are not. There are more than seventy of them to choose from and they're actually gaining in popularity—admissions have been up in recent years.

Concerns about a restricted social life and limited dating opportunities prevent many young women from considering women's colleges. But, there are some compelling reasons why a college-bound gal might want to add them to her list of possibilities. Only about two percent of all female college students graduate from women's colleges, but a very large percentage of the graduates of these schools end up in some top positions.

For example, check out the following statistics, as cited by Converse College and **www.WomensColleges.org**.

Graduates of all-female colleges represent:

- 20% of the women in Congress
- 20% of *Fortune* magazine's 50 Most Powerful Women in American Business
- 33% of female board members for Fortune 1000 companies
- 50% of the women pursuing advanced degrees
- 30% of *Business Week's* 50 women who are rising stars in corporate America

Why are those who attend women's colleges so successful? One reason often cited is that women can focus more on challenging themselves intellectually because they are free of the distractions of dating. Also, there are more opportunities for women to assume leadership roles. This is not to say that such opportunities for female students are absent in co-ed schools, but at all-female colleges women fill 100% of these roles. They also fill the majority of jobs there: 90% of the presidents and 55% of the faculty are women.

Despite all these stats, it's important to remember that there are millions of female students who thrive in a co-ed environment and prefer to be around both sexes because that's what it's like in the real world.

> *"I think an all women's school is fantastic. It's a great opportunity. But I have a lot of friends who went to Smith and it just seems like oftentimes when they get out, they're just really naïve when it comes to the ways of the world."*

> **Recent Grad,
> Wheaton College**

THE BEST OF BOTH WORLDS

by
Margo Dobbertin
Recent Grad, Barnard College

I applied to Barnard because I liked the idea of a women's college but wanted the resources and environment of a larger university. However, I enrolled for slightly different reasons, namely, that I wanted to be in New York City, and because, ultimately, Barnard offered me slightly more money than the small, Midwestern liberal arts college that was my second choice.

As with any college search, I think the most important task is to visit early on and keep in mind what you want out of your college experience. Try to discover the tenor and personality of the school and its student body, be honest with yourself regarding your motivations, and prepare to be flexible. For example, a women's college (especially in a rural area), could mean a stilted dating environment, an ideal dating environment, or an opportunity for undistracted study, depending on your personal perspective.

CREATE YOUR IDEAL COLLEGE PROFILE

Now that you've considered the many aspects of college life you're probably starting to get a clearer idea of what your ideal college could be like. It really helps to create a chart, and on the next page we've included one as an example. You can use this template or create your own—the main idea is to have something that will serve as your guide as you dive into researching schools. Having an idea of what you want will make the search process much easier.

On the left-hand side, list the different aspects of college life—for example, academic offerings or cost. Then, next to each point, write what you would like ideally in that area. Make sure you include all the areas that are important to you. Finally, figure out how important each particular aspect is. We've created columns for you to mark each characteristic as "must have," "nice to have," or "not critical." When you start to look at actual colleges, you'll want to focus on finding those with the most "must have" qualities. Just don't mark them all as "must have."

An ideal college profile can be a helpful guide in your college search, but try not to feel bound by it. Your priorities may and probably will change, and that's okay. Keep an open mind and remember that some college may have this great program about which you didn't even know and with which you might fall in love.

"I always thought that I'd major in econ, but then I visited Wesleyan and learned about this combined major called the College of Social Studies. It included some econ, some government and history, and even some philosophy. As I learned more about it, I couldn't think of anything else that appealed to me more."

**Recent Grad,
Wesleyan University**

	What you want in each area	How important is this particular characteristic?		
		Must have	Nice to have	Not Critical
Academic Offerings	Good comp. lit., film, and English departments.	X		
Admission Difficulty	Medium to hard.	X		
Academic Tone	Challenging, but not so that I'll completely lose it.	X		
Special Programs & Offerings	Good study abroad program.		X	
Cost	Not much money from folks, so need scholarship or not super-expensive.	X		
Size	Medium to large campus.		X	
Location	Urban or college town. Definitely not rural! Prefer Northeast.	X		
Social Tone	Diverse, liberal, socially aware students. Fun, but not party school.		X	
Particular Orientation	Grew up Episcopalian, but do I care?			X

"Remember that there's a good place for everyone. In fact, there are lots of good college fits for every student who wants to go to college. So my advice is not to limit your possibilities. Look at colleges big and small, rural and urban, universities and liberal arts colleges, and every other variation. And remember that you can get a terrific education at virtually any place where you're willing and eager to work hard."

President,
Haverford College

6

research your potential schools

There are tons of resources you can use to find out more about colleges. Like any good researcher, you don't want to rely too heavily on any one source of information or you'll end up with a biased view. Make your search as broad as possible without overwhelming yourself.

Also, as you begin your search, try to keep an open mind and free yourself from any prejudices or pre-conceived notions you may have about particular schools. Many more schools than the Ivy League colleges offer stellar academics, and just because a college is a highly competitive one doesn't mean that students are boring and don't know how to have a good time.

HAVE A PLAN
▼
TALK WITH YOUR GUIDANCE COUNSELOR
▼
LEARN FROM STUDENTS AND ALUMS
▼
TAKE ADVANTAGE OF COLLEGE FAIRS
▼
CONSIDER SCHOOL RANKINGS
▼
CHECK OUT A FEW GUIDEBOOKS
▼
READ THROUGH SCHOOL MATERIALS
▼
USE THE WEB
▼
DON'T NEGLECT YOUR PARENTS
▼
KEEP GOOD NOTES

HAVE A PLAN

Before you dive into your research, you need to have some kind of a plan. Otherwise, before you know it, you'll be drowning in piles of papers and have no idea why you were even looking at a particular college in the first place. Use your ideal college profile, have an organized approach for looking at each school, and think about how many schools you'll need to research.

> *"I'd written down the few things that were most important to me in a college—strong econ department, small campus, near a city—and kept this piece of paper with me as I researched schools. It was a great reminder."*
>
> **Recent Grad,**
> **Wesleyan University**

As we mentioned in our college timeline, try to start your college research at the beginning of your junior year. That way you'll have enough time to look at a few schools, decide which ones to visit, and even re-visit some if you feel you need to. If you can avoid being rushed, it's a huge help.

Start your research by looking at your ideal college profile and identifying a few of the most important qualities you'd like your college to have. If you know you want a good history department, start by looking at some schools that have one. If you're after a tough academic environment, that can be your starting point. Or, if you know you want a college in California that's a top academic school you can use those two qualities combined to start your search.

Once you've identified a bunch of schools—say ten to twenty—that have one or more of your top requirements, see how they measure up in the other areas that are important to you. Make note of any that seem to hit the mark in several areas. These are the ones you'll want to research in more depth.

Depending on what you're looking for, you may come up with either too few or too many schools and will have to broaden or narrow your search. If you want to go to college in Arizona and you also want to major in Finnish, you're probably not going to come up with that many schools that meet both of those requirements. Pick what's more important to you—Finnish major or Arizona—and broaden your search based on that change. On the other hand, if you want to study English at a school in the Northeast, you're going to come up with way too many schools to consider in depth. To narrow down your search, add another requirement. For example, if you'd like a quiet campus, you can research schools with good English programs in rural campuses in the Northeast.

Another useful technique we've found is to have a system for looking at each school as you go through your research. It doesn't have to be anything complicated, but find a way that works for you and use it consistently. Maybe you start by looking at the school's website, then read a few guidebooks, and then talk to some alums. Or perhaps you can start by reading the school's brochures and course catalogues, and then move on to the web. If it works for you, it works!

WE TALK WITH...

Patty McKeever
Recent Grad, Wheaton College

In looking at colleges, what appealed to you the most about the college you eventually chose?

It had a strong English major and I liked the professors. It was also good to be close to home and it was a great campus.

If you could do it over again, would you pick the same school?

If I had to do it again I would be less naïve about what it's like to come out of school as a theater major. My education didn't come to fruition as I hoped it would. It never taught us that professional edge. I probably would've gone to a school like NYU—I think they have a lot more theater students and theater professors.

Why do you think you ended up going to a school that wasn't quite right for what you wanted?

I don't think I researched schools as in depth as I should have. This was one of the first schools that I looked at. I looked at Wheaton, Brown, and Wellesley, and I just really liked Wheaton. I think I should've done more research and looked at more schools—I got a little over-zealous. I applied early, got accepted, and then couldn't apply to other places.

Are there any mistakes you think you made in doing college research?

It's easy to get romanced by the teacher-to-student ratio. There were fifteen students to one professor, but that meant with thirty students in the theater major there were only two professors!

TALK WITH YOUR GUIDANCE COUNSELOR

High school counselors are a great resource when it comes to learning about colleges, financial aid, and admissions-related information. They can tell you about particular schools, as well as the specific requirements for getting into them. They can also tell you about many useful and relevant college-search resources.

The more prepared you are in terms of knowing what you want, the better your guidance counselor will be able to help you. You shouldn't feel shy about asking for help, even if you're an all-knowing superstar. Guidance counselors have years of experience in this area and there are also side benefits to establishing a good relationship with them: They can be a great reference if they know you well and they have significant influence over some scholarship money that you're after.

Below are some questions you might want to ask your counselor as you discuss your potential college choices:

- Are my grades good enough to get into this college?
- I want to go to this school that's tough to get into. Do you think I should take more advanced placement courses?
- How can I find out more about this particular school?
- Do you think this college is worth a visit?
- Which of these two colleges do you think would be better for me?
- Has anyone from our school ever gone to this college? Do you know how I could get in touch with them?
- My parents think I wouldn't be happy at this school. What do you think?
- Do you think this school is challenging enough for me?
- Do you think the information in this guidebook is accurate?

- Are there any scholarships I should be looking into?
- This college offers a major I'm really interested in, but I'm not used to that kind of setting. Do you think I would adjust easily?
- My parents won't be contributing that much financially and I'm kind of freaked out about borrowing a lot of money, but I want to go to a really good school. What are my options?

As with all advice that you get during this process—and if your experience is anything like ours, you'll get a lot—know that it's just the opinion of one person or one source. Don't rely on it like it's the law and be strong enough to make your own judgments.

LEARN FROM STUDENTS AND ALUMS

"One of my friends had been at this school for a semester and another friend for a year. They both were really helpful. They were able to tell me what to expect from the campus as a whole, the student body, and the professors, as well as what the atmosphere of the campus and town was like."

Recent Grad,
Southwest Texas State University

Alumni and current students at a college can be extremely valuable sources of information. They've been there and can give you first-hand accounts of their experiences. Ask them questions about class experience, social issues, or other things that concern you. Talking with them can also give you a sense of what types of students attend this school and how comfortable you'll be interacting with them.

Another benefit of alumni and current students is that unlike counselors, college representatives, and your parents, they are your peers—or at least much closer to your age—and you may feel more comfortable asking them certain types of questions.

Siobhan's corner

▼

Right around the time I was considering Columbia, I met a woman who was going there. She was an English major with a minor in writing, which, funny enough, ended up being my major and minor. She was really down-to-earth and outgoing and I remember thinking that if the other students there were like her, I'd fit right in. She was very happy with her choice of college and had nothing but good things to say about it. I was really interested in hearing about the writing classes, and so it was great to hear about them from someone who had taken more than a few. She said they were great. Getting first-hand information from someone I really related to helped me feel confident about my choice.

▲

Remember that what current students and alumni tell you is highly subjective. Just because they had a certain experience doesn't mean that you'll have the same one. For example, if someone tells you, "It's hard to make friends here," it may be that this person is not very outgoing and hasn't made an effort to make friends.

GETTING THE REAL DEAL

by
Aimee Zygmonski
Recent Grad, Emerson College

Getting the real information about the schools where I applied was one of the most important aspects of my college search. Because I was applying to performing arts schools, I was looking for a different type of education than a regular liberal arts school offers. I wanted to know specifics: how good were certain faculty members, how was the level of talent within the student body, how many graduates went on to professional theater and did well, and was the level of training really worth the tuition bill? Sure, the college had numbers, percentages, and literature that was graphically pleasing and professional, but I wanted more.

Luckily, I met a current student at Emerson who was able to sit with me for an hour and talk frankly about the program. You know those scholarships that the university talks about offering? Don't even think about it. But a certain advisor will try her hardest to get you the money that you deserve—as long as you work hard. You know that teacher that the university is so proud of? Don't even bother taking his class. But the new faculty member—oh yes!—she's amazing and you should take all her classes.

Getting the real deal on classes, how the university works, financial aid, etc. was invaluable in helping me make my final decision in choosing a college. Remember, not only are universities interviewing you, but you are interviewing them. They want all the information they can find about you. As a prospective student, you have a right to learn as much as you can about them.

TAKE ADVANTAGE OF COLLEGE FAIRS

College fairs can be useful because they allow you to talk to admissions representatives from numerous colleges in one location in a short period of time. They're usually held at high schools or large conference spaces and typically take place during the spring for juniors and in the fall for seniors.

Because there's so much going on at these fairs and many pieces of information to collect, it's important to prepare beforehand and go in with a strategy. If you don't, it's all too easy to get lost in the hustle and bustle.

▶BEFORE YOU GO

- Get a list of the colleges that will be represented and decide which you'd like to visit. Then, do some preliminary research about these schools before you go—this way you can ask the representatives informed questions.

- Get a layout of the fair and map out your route. Figure out how many tables you want to visit and in what order you'll see them. Make sure you leave time for just hanging around and browsing a bit.

- Get a schedule of any information sessions. These usually cover topics like the application process, financial aid, and other things to help you in your college search.

- Come up with a list of questions to ask. Try to think of questions that can't be answered from reading about the schools. Don't ask: "What majors do you offer?"—you can easily find this out in a guidebook or online. Instead, you could ask about specific courses that you'd take as part of a major and what the professors are like within that major.

▶THINGS TO TAKE WITH YOU

- Your list of questions.

- A large bag for all the material you'll be collecting.

- A notebook and pen so that after you leave a table, you can write down your impressions before going on to the next one. If you don't write things down immediately, the schools may all start to blend together.

- A bunch of self-adhesive address labels so that you don't have to keep filling out your name again and again at every table.

- Your parents. If one of your parents comes with you, you should plan a strategy together. If you have a lot of territory to cover and you're worried about time, you can split up. One of you could go to an information session while the other goes to the college tables. Sticking together can be useful, too. Sometimes your parents will ask questions that hadn't occurred to you.

At some point after you leave the fair, look through the materials you gathered and start organizing it. If it turns out you ended up with material from a college that doesn't look so hot, get rid of it—you don't need it cluttering up your life. For the schools that seem interesting, decide what additional information you want to get from them and then file their materials in the appropriate folders.

"It's very easy to get caught up in the name game and to try to play that game. A lot of happy and productive people in the world didn't go to Harvard. Many people choose to go to colleges that are much less competitive and find an opportunity to grow and develop better as people."

Director of College Counseling,
Lakeside School

CONSIDER SCHOOL RANKINGS

The most popular rankings are probably <u>America's Best Colleges</u> put out by U.S. News and World Report. Rankings tell you how schools measure up to one another, both overall and in terms of particular departments. They can be a good starting point in your search. For example, if you know you want to go to a school with a good anthropology department, you can consult the rankings to see which schools are the best in this area. It's a lot easier than randomly investigating colleges that might not even have this as a major. You may even come across schools that hadn't occurred to you.

College rankings are also useful to get an idea about admission difficulty and where you stand compared to the average student at the school. They tell you about acceptance and retention rates, test scores of entering students, and overall student body demographics.

It's important to realize the limitations of rankings. Much more than just academic strength goes into a ranking—the level of alumni donations, for example—so just because a school is ranked in the top ten overall doesn't mean that its academics alone are top-ten quality. Also, overall rankings don't tell you much about specific departments. Even if a school is not ranked highly, it might have several strong majors, and if these majors are what you're looking for, it would be a shame to discount the school.

> *"Don't read too much into the 'US News Top 50' college rankings—they don't mean that much. Read guidebooks that talk about what the colleges are really like. Then you can decide which ones are right for you."*
>
> **Junior,**
> **Millsaps College**

How much attention you should pay to college rankings is a point of contention—some people think a lot, some people think less. Our main advice here is to consider rankings as just another piece of information about a college: Don't rely on them too much, but don't ignore them either.

CHECK OUT A FEW GUIDEBOOKS

"Although college guides, such as The Best 331 Colleges, are excellent for your college search, don't take them as scripture. Visiting campuses will give you the best impression of campus life."

**Freshman,
Fairfield University**

There are a lot of different guidebooks from which you can choose. In general, it's best to look at those that are updated annually. Things change and you want the most current information.

The more objective guidebooks, such as the Complete Book of Colleges, (Princeton Review, published every year), provide basic information about colleges, such as the academic programs available, requirements for admission, student demographics, cost of attendance, and so on. There are also more subjective guidebooks, such as The Fiske Guide to Colleges, (Sourcebooks Trade, published every year), which offer opinions on the colleges they profile. They comment on things like quality of campus life, the effect of the location on student life, the strengths and weaknesses of different academic programs, and academic and social tone. Although they usually gather information from a large number of students and educators at the schools they profile, subjective guidebooks are just that—

subjective. While it can be useful to see what students think about a particular school, keep in mind that other people who didn't get interviewed might disagree completely with the opinions offered about their colleges.

You might disagree, too. Remember, guidebooks weren't written specifically with you in mind and can't possibly know what you're looking for. They are well worth reading, and whatever they do have to say you can either validate or invalidate later by talking with your counselor or other students, and by visiting the schools and seeing for yourself.

Siobhan's corner
▼

When I first started thinking about college, I went to the bookstore and impulsively bought a couple of books that I thought I'd definitely need to help me in my search. Parts of them were pretty helpful, but there was a lot of information I still needed that they didn't cover. This meant more books. It dawned on me that this could get expensive, so I decided to use some library resources. There were some books that I found myself coming back to again and again, so I bought those. With others, there was just a chapter or a few pages that were useful. For those I just Xeroxed the pages I needed and filed the information away. I saved a lot of money.
▲

READ THROUGH SCHOOL MATERIALS

Your high school may have printed materials from various colleges. If it doesn't, you can request materials directly from the college's admissions office. Keep in mind that materials supplied by a college are marketing aids designed to generate your interest in the school.

Even so, there is a lot to be learned from reading them. Pay attention to what the college emphasizes about itself, what majors are offered, the various rules and requirements, and the overall tone. Figure out what's near the college and what the housing arrangements are.

You should also request the school's course catalogue. This is the best source of information on what types of classes are offered and can help you figure out if this is the kind of curriculum that you can get excited about.

It's also a good idea to get a copy of the school's newspaper. Because students write the paper, it can give you a really good idea of what the student body is like. Pay attention to what things are highlighted, what kinds of issues are discussed, and what activities are taking place. This is a great way to get a feel for what the day-to-day is like at each college you're considering.

USE THE WEB

The Internet is a great resource and can save you a lot of time, legwork, and money. You can use it to search for colleges based on several characteristics, take virtual college tours, request college information, and much more. Here are a few of our favorite web resources, but check the "**helpful resources**" section at the end of this book for more ideas:

www.CollegeBoard.org has a tool to help you make quick, side-by-side comparisons of two or three colleges, as well as a tool for comparing financial aid awards.

www.WiredScholar.com lets you search for colleges using several criteria and also has many useful checklists that you can print out and use.

It's also helpful to check out the websites of the colleges you're considering. Here's some information that you can find there:

- History of the school
- Mission of the school
- Majors offered
- How and when to apply
- How many students apply and how many are accepted
- Stats on accepted students (class rank, GPA, etc.)
- Stats on student body (ethnicity, religion, gender, etc.)
- Financial aid statistics
- Online/printable applications
- Housing options
- Dining facilities
- Clubs and organizations
- Volunteer opportunities
- Sports
- Academic calendar
- Map of campus
- Campus tours
- Visual images of campus
- Virtual tours

DON'T NEGLECT YOUR PARENTS

Parents can be great resources. You can bounce ideas off them because they know you really well and have your best interests at heart. They're great for practical stuff, too, because they've probably been through the college search process before—even though it was quite some time ago.

"My parents helped keep me organized. During senior year you have all this stuff going on and it's really easy to lose track of where you are in the college process. My parents kept me on track and reminded me about where I needed to be."

Junior,
Vassar College

KEEP GOOD NOTES

Keeping good notes as you plow through tons of college information will make your life a lot easier. If you spend a couple of hours reading up on a school, write down any important points you'd like to remember. After you've read up on several schools they may start to blend together.

Don't let pieces of paper scribbled with website addresses and phone numbers pile up. Put them in the files of the appropriate schools so that you can find them easily. In your own books, catalogs, and other printed materials, underlining or highlighting important information and then flagging the page with a Post-it note is a great way to help you find information quickly when you need it.

Keep your ideal college profile nearby as you research colleges and refer to it from time to time to see if any of your priorities have changed. Don't feel like you have to stick to your original requirements—the purpose of all of this research is to learn more about what you need in a college, and if that changes, that's totally fine.

7

make the most of campus visits

If at all possible, you should visit any school you're seriously considering. No matter how much you read about a college or find out from other people who've gone there, there is no substitute for visiting. Actually being on campus and soaking in the atmosphere is the closest you can get to being part of a college and knowing what it's like to actually go there.

DECIDE WHICH COLLEGES TO VISIT
▼
FIGURE OUT THE BEST TIME TO GO
▼
CHOOSE YOUR COMPANION CAREFULLY
▼
PREPARE FOR YOUR VISIT
▼
TAKE A TOUR
▼
STAY OVERNIGHT
▼
MAKE THE MOST OF YOUR TIME ON CAMPUS
▼
ASK LOTS OF QUESTIONS
▼
WRITE DOWN YOUR IMPRESSIONS

DECIDE WHICH COLLEGES TO VISIT

"I'd never been to Ohio when I packed up all my stuff in California and moved here. I don't think I would change going to Ohio University, but I think I came with different expectations."

Junior,
Ohio University

There's no formula for figuring out how many and which colleges to visit. Ideally, you'd visit every school you're thinking about, but this is rarely possible because of time constraints and travel expenses that can add up. So you have to narrow down your list.

One way to do this is to visit schools "virtually" first. Some colleges will send you a video tour of the campus, which can be helpful, but this is mostly a representation of what the college wants its image to be. There are independent virtual tour companies, like **www.CampusTours.com**, that aggregate virtual tours produced by colleges and make it easier for you to see a few of them in one place. A virtual tour is no substitute for the real thing, but it can help you decide which schools to visit in person.

Another way to narrow down your list is to focus on colleges where you're on the fence. If you keep thinking about one or two schools but can't decide if you should apply there, a visit can help clarify your choices.

We'll talk later about making sure that you apply to a variety of schools in terms of difficulty, and as you think of where to visit, make sure that your list includes some reach as well as some safety colleges. And if you're thinking of applying somewhere Early Decision, visiting that school is a must.

SPENDING A DAY AND NIGHT ON CAMPUS

by
Emily Regas
Recent Grad, University of California - Santa Barbara

Visiting the campus of each and every school I applied to was a key factor in my decision-making process. While glossy brochures filled with smiling students made each campus seem like a warm, inviting community that was just right for me, I really didn't know exactly what environment I wanted to live in for the next four years until I experienced it. When asked, most campuses had opportunities to spend an entire day there, sitting in on classes, speaking to admissions counselors, taking tours, and just experiencing everything the campus had to offer. The size of the campus, how students got from class to class, even the places students study were important factors in realizing which campus would feel like home.

What impressed me the most about my college visits was how the preconceptions of what I thought I wanted in a school were laid to rest after I spent an entire day there. At the University of California - Santa Barbara I really experienced freshman life by spending time with students in their dorm room. I was able to speak to current students, ask questions about dorm life, and see if I could really live in their residence halls. I attended some classes I thought I'd potentially like to take and ate most of my meals in the dining commons so I could get a feel for a student's daily life. During the tour I asked the guide where students spent their free time and I visited some of the local coffee shops and popular study spots. Ultimately this was the school for me, but I wouldn't have come to that conclusion if I hadn't spent the day there experiencing everything the campus and the surrounding community had to offer.

FIGURE OUT THE BEST TIME TO GO

The best time to visit a college is when things are in full swing. You can still learn a lot even when students are on vacation, but it's not the same as visiting it during the hustle and bustle of a regular day on campus.

For this reason, you shouldn't plan all of your visits in the middle of the summer or over the Thanksgiving or Christmas holidays (when most schools are actually closed). High school holidays are a great time for visits, especially during spring vacation. National holidays that fall on a Monday are another good time, as not all colleges have these days off. Just make sure to check with the specific colleges you're visiting.

Try not to plan visits during college reading weeks or exam periods. Students are very busy then, and even if they're not cloistered in the library, they may not have time for questions or be as friendly as they would be during less stressful times. During this time you may not be able to sit in on classes and that's an important component of every campus visit.

You should definitely try to visit some colleges before applications are due between November and March of your senior year (depending on whether you're applying early or not). Keep in mind that decision notices arrive in mid-April and your reply is required by most colleges by May 1st. This means that if you wait until after you're accepted, you may only have two weeks for campus visits.

Kate McCulley
Freshman, Fairfield University

When do you think is the best time to visit colleges?

People tell you that the best time to go is during your junior year, and they're right. By junior year you should have a good idea of what you want in a college, and you'll be able to visit without the time crunch of senior year.

What are the best and worst times during the year to go?

Spring is the best time to go—just make sure that it isn't during college spring break! Other times to avoid are during midterms, finals, and other times of the year when the atmosphere at college might not be as amiable as you would expect it to be. While summer might seem like a great time to visit, this actually isn't true because most students won't be around. During a visit you should talk to as many students as possible, and you can't do that during the summer!

If you're crunched for time, try visiting schools during a long weekend. In addition to missing only one day of school, you'll get to see what the weekend life is like at the college you're visiting. It's good to know what people do outside of classes.

CHOOSE YOUR COMPANION CAREFULLY

Your experience visiting a campus will probably be very different depending on who is with you, or if you're alone. Parents can be good to bring along for both emotional and financial support. They can help you get organized and arrange the details of the trip, and they sometimes think of things to investigate on campus that may not even occur to you.

> *"Having my parents with me during college visits was great for me. I was really nervous, so it was comforting to have some support. I think they also liked being involved in the process. It gave them the chance to share their input about things that they thought would be good for me."*
>
> **Recent Grad,**
> **Vassar College**

On the flip side, if your parents are being a bit overbearing in the college search process, you might want to spend some time visiting colleges on your own or with a friend. That way, you'll have a chance to make up your own mind.

Visiting colleges with your best friend might seem very appealing, but you should only go to colleges in which you're really interested. The two of you may have different priorities and to visit colleges that don't meet yours is a waste of your already-limited time.

If you do choose to go with a friend or a group of friends, remember to treat the visit seriously. That doesn't mean that you can't have fun, but you should stay focused. Your mission is to find out as much as you can about the place where you could potentially be spending the next several years of your life.

"On my first visit I went with my mom and my best friend. Having the combination of the two was great because my friend knows me really well and my mom had a mature outlook on the whole thing. For the second trip, I traveled alone and visited friends who were already in college. That was really fun, but it wasn't as helpful because it became more of a social visit and I wasn't as focused. I think you get a skewed perspective when you're visiting friends."

**Recent Grad,
Vassar College**

Making a visit alone also has some advantages. First of all, your agenda is your own. You can stroll around campus at your leisure without the pressure of having anyone waiting for you. Also, it can give you a real feeling of what it would be like to be there without family or friends from home.

If you really don't want to go alone and can't find anyone to go with you, let your guidance counselor know that you're looking for a traveling partner or see if you can post a notice in the guidance counselor's office to meet up with someone else.

PREPARE FOR YOUR VISIT

Before you visit, call the admissions office and get some information. They will be able to tell you the best time to come and will help arrange for a campus tour or a place to stay overnight. Also, if you want to meet with a particular professor or coach, you should book an appointment well ahead of time.

Before you leave home, make sure you have everything you need. If you've scheduled an interview you should bring the appropriate clothing. Also, make sure you have the address of the college and directions on how to get there, as well as the names and phone numbers of anyone you need to see.

Bring a notebook and pen for anything you may want to write down. And, most importantly, bring lots of questions. It's a great idea to write them down in advance so that you don't forget to ask something you really wanted to know.

> *"I gave tours at Vassar and had prospective students pull me aside and ask me about the drug scene and the party scene. It's important to ask those types of questions if that's something that concerns you. You can ask about the dating scene, the work load, satisfaction with majors, anything, but it's important to ask your own questions, not your parents'."*

**Recent Grad,
Vassar College**

TAKE A TOUR

"It was raining the day I visited Vassar. We had umbrellas and we were walking around from building to building. The thing that they said that I thought was great was: 'If you love Vassar on a rainy day you'll love it even more on a sunny day.' And I think that's true. Even though it was raining, I still thought it was a gorgeous campus."

**Recent Grad,
Vassar College**

Taking a campus tour is a great way to be introduced to the college. You'll get to hear about the history of the college and see all the important sites like the library, classrooms, dorms, dean's office, dining halls, and sports facilities. Your guide might take you to places you hadn't thought to check out or didn't know about. Later on, you can wander aimlessly if you want, or go back to any areas you saw on the tour that you want to investigate further.

THE ULTIMATE TEST DRIVE

by
Owen Confliti
Recent Grad, Emerson College

I had a vision of what Emerson would be like, but not how I'd feel actually being there and living in Boston. The tour was the ultimate test drive. My student guide and I spent the afternoon building-hopping, exploring the campus, and talking to students and professors. We did everything but eat in the cafeteria—and that was a good thing.

Broadcasting was my thing, so the school's media classes and facilities were most important. The college radio station was cozy. It had character. It also had the latest digital editing system! Since I'd never seen a real TV studio before, I was in shock. Someday I'd learn what all those buttons, knobs, and lights did. To top it off, everyone looked like they were having fun. I was sold on the atmosphere.

But there was more to consider. Boston is a dynamic city with lots of energy. The weather is unpredictable. My first night was cold and windy with freezing rain. This was just a regular December day for the locals. For me, it was tolerable and temporary. I wouldn't let it scare me off. Massachusetts has four seasons, unlike other parts of New England criticized for only having two: winter and July.

There was only so much I could get from the big college handbook or the school's information package. I needed to walk the halls, mingle with the students, and be part of the action. It felt right. My search was over. Now all I had to worry about was being accepted!

STAY OVERNIGHT

If you can, plan to stay overnight during at least a few college visits. Just as you want to know what a campus is like on a busy school day, you also want to get a sense of what it's like at night. You'll usually room with a current student, and there's no better way to get to know the student body and what people are really like.

It's a great idea to spend the evening at some sort of event that interests you, whether sporting, cultural, social, or something else. Meet as many students as you can and try not to be shy about it. Now that we're college students we know that we actually like talking to prospective students like you—it makes us feel important!

However you decide to spend your time, make sure that when night falls, you take the time to walk around campus, paying attention to how it feels. Is there loud music? Is it deserted? Do you feel safe? These are all important impressions to take into account.

"I saw one school that on paper looked absolutely amazing. When I got there, even though the campus itself was beautiful, I didn't feel safe outside of campus, which was a huge thing for me, especially being so far away from home. So I didn't apply there."

**Recent Grad,
Adelphi University**

MY FIRST VISIT TO YALE

by
Amy Herzog
Recent Grad, Yale University

My brother is three years older than I am, and when I tagged along on his college visits I decided, somewhat arbitrarily, that I wanted to go to Yale. When my own senior year rolled around and my choice of what college to attend became a reality instead of just something I said, it occurred to me that I should spend some time on campus before sending in my application for Early Decision.

I didn't know anyone who went to Yale and had no sense of the student body or the social life. I signed up to stay on campus overnight and got hooked up with a suite full of first-year women who had volunteered to host prospective students. Because it was only November at the time of my visit, my hosts themselves were still getting to know Yale and finding their footing, socially and academically. I was most impressed by their huge variety of interests and the basic warmth with which they greeted me and treated each other. They took me out for pizza, let me in on all kinds of campus and dorm gossip, and helped to set me up with friends who were taking the classes I was most interested in visiting the following day. As it turned out, I was less enthusiastic about the two classes I visited than about the students who accompanied me there. But I figured that at Yale, like any other university, there would be tremendous professors and less than tremendous professors, great classes and mediocre classes.

What mattered to me then was that I was around curious, outgoing, and interesting people with whom I'd be happy to spend four years. Spending time with students overnight—when they had a break from classes and spent down time together—gave me a necessary glimpse of what I was getting into. I applied early, was accepted, and had a great time!

MAKE THE MOST OF YOUR TIME ON CAMPUS

"It's very easy to build something up into an idea, but when you see it, it's never exactly what you thought it was going to be. With visits, you get a real tangible feel for the possibilities of a place that you just don't get on paper."

**Recent Grad,
Columbia University**

There is a lot to take in when you visit a campus, so to make the most of your time, figure out what you definitely want to see and do before you get there. Here are some suggestions:

✓ Classrooms
✓ Departments that interest you
✓ Study areas
✓ Dorms
✓ Dining halls
✓ Student-activity centers
✓ Computer facilities
✓ Athletic facilities
✓ Career counseling office
✓ Health facilities
✓ Assembly halls
✓ Performance spaces and movie theaters
✓ School clubs
✓ Outdoor areas
✓ Science labs
✓ Administrative offices

As well as walking around and looking at things, you might want to round out your visit by doing some of the following:

✓ Taking a tour
✓ Having an interview
✓ Sitting in on a class
✓ Eating in the dining facilities
✓ Sleeping in a dorm
✓ Talking to professors
✓ Talking to students
✓ Attending a cultural event
✓ Attending a sporting event

"Go into the dorms and look around. Some of them are not bad, but some of them are scary. I think it's important to see all the aspects."

Recent Grad,
Abilene Christian University

You won't be spending all your time on campus when you go to college, so make sure you investigate what's nearby. Spend some time in the local town or community and get a feel for what it's like and what types of facilities and activities it offers.

Some things you might want to check out are:

✓ Movie and other theaters
✓ Shops
✓ Restaurants
✓ Public transportation
✓ Clubs and music venues
✓ Museums
✓ Parks and recreational areas
✓ Banks

"Visiting campuses opened my eyes more than anything else. Upon arrival at one particularly large urban campus, I was so repulsed by the decrepit facilities and lack of security that I didn't even show up for my guided tour the next day."

**Freshman,
Fairfield University**

☞ **SAMPLE COLLEGE VISIT ITINERARY**

Friday Night
- Arrive and check into hotel or dorm
- Eat in school dining facilities
- Hang out in the dorm and talk to students

Saturday Morning
- Have breakfast at a different dining facility
- Take your pre-arranged guided tour

Saturday Afternoon
- Have lunch with your student buddy
- Walk around campus and go back to anything on your "must see" list not covered on the tour

Saturday Night
- Have dinner at a college hangout near the school
- Go hear a band at a local club

Sunday Morning
- Have breakfast at the local diner
- Walk around town and get a feel for the place

Sunday Afternoon
- Have lunch in town
- Go to a local park or check out local scenery

Sunday Night
- Eat dinner at the pizza place on campus
- Go back to the dorm for an early night

Monday Morning
- Ace your interview with admissions staff

Monday Afternoon
- Eat lunch on campus
- Sit in on a class
- Talk to professors in departments of interest to you

ASK LOTS OF QUESTIONS

"During my visit, I talked to many of the professors and sat in on a few classes. I'm really glad I came up here several times—I really feel like I made the right decision."

**Recent Grad,
Southwest Texas State University**

While on campus ask as many questions as you can of as many people as you can. Talk to the students, the admissions staff, and your tour guides. It's also a really good idea to talk to professors who teach subjects that interest you. You can ask about the courses, the workload, and what typical assignments are like. It's also really important to get a sense of whether these are people from whom you can learn: Are they enthusiastic? Energetic? Knowledgeable? Accessible?

Students are one of your best sources of information. They are more likely to know what might be important to you, and because they don't have a vested interest in you attending the school, they'll be more willing to tell you about any of the less desirable elements. The best students to talk to are usually those with whom you share either an academic or recreational interest. If you're interested in theater, find out where the theater classes meet, hang around in that area, and strike up conversations. If you're athletic and you see someone coming out of the gym, approach him or her for a chat.

Talking to students will not only provide you with information about various aspects of campus life but will also give you an idea of what the students themselves are like. As you talk to them, try to gauge their attitudes on various topics and how you feel talking to them. You want to figure out if these are the kinds of people with whom you'd enjoy spending lots of time and who could become your friends.

WRITE DOWN YOUR IMPRESSIONS

You'll probably visit at least a few schools and because there's so much to take in at each one, it's a good idea to take notes. If you don't, the many schools you visit may all start to mix together. The best time to record your experiences is either during your visit or right afterwards while things are still fresh in your mind.

> *"The most useful thing was coming out here, even though it was only for a day. You obviously can't glean that much from one day, but a lot of judgments I made on that day turned out to be right."*
>
> **Recent Grad,**
> **UCLA**

GOOD QUESTIONS TO ASK STUDENTS

- What are the best and worst things about this college?
- Has the college lived up to your expectations?
- Have you been happy with the college overall?
- How strong is the (underline your interest) department?
- How challenging is the school?
- How is the grading system?
- How much time do students typically spend studying?
- What is the workload like?
- What are the classes like?
- What is the tone like in smaller classes?
- How easy or difficult is it to get into the classes you want to take?
- What are the professors like?
- What's the social atmosphere like?
- Is the student population diverse?
- Have you made good friends?
- Do you feel supported at the college?
- What are the dorms like?
- What is there to do on campus?
- What's the atmosphere like on campus at night?
- Which are the best places to eat on campus?
- Is the campus safe at night?
- What is there to do in town?
- What's nearby that's worth checking out?

"I'm a great believer in gut reactions. I think when you visit a college, spend some time there, talk to students and professors, see what life is like—you get a basic sense of whether you fit in or not, whether you think you'd like to study here."

**Assistant Dean of Liberal Arts and Sciences,
Northwestern University**

8

decide where
to apply

You've researched the colleges and you've visited some of them. The time has now come for you to decide where you're going to apply. This may seem kind of scary—it's all so final. But you've done a lot of work to find out what you want out of a college and what colleges are out there and you're in a great position to make an informed decision.

In this chapter we've put together some suggestions for how to turn your research and knowledge about what you're after and what colleges you're considering into a list of colleges where you're going to apply.

COMPARE AND CONTRAST COLLEGES
▼
DIVERSIFY YOUR CHOICES
▼
THINK ABOUT EARLY DECISION
▼
GET FEEDBACK

COMPARE AND CONTRAST COLLEGES

Using your ideal college profile—which has probably changed somewhat during your research—and all the material you've gathered about various colleges, you should take some time to compare and contrast your potential choices. The number of colleges you evaluate will vary depending on your individual circumstances and needs. But at this point you should probably have at least ten so that there is room to discard some. As a general rule, if you have more than fifteen, try to eliminate some by doing a bit more thinking and research.

"First I looked at schools based on my major and then I started narrowing it down—I originally had thirty schools. Then I did the next cut using special services as my guideline. This brought it down to ten. Location was the next thing. Being in theater, I didn't feel that going to a school out in the middle of nowhere was the best thing for me. I ended up looking at schools around Chicago and New York and that pretty much narrowed it down to six."

**Recent Grad,
Adelphi University**

A great way to make comparisons is to put together a simple chart. We've included one as an example at the end of this section. In the left column, list the college characteristics that are important to you. (Use your ideal college profile!) Across the top row, list the colleges you're considering. In the appropriate space, simply check below any college that satisfies that particular characteristic. If you want to go a step further, you can use numbers instead of checkmarks to create a ranking system. Use numbers from 0 to 3, with 3 satisfying a given point completely, 2 satisfying it fairly well, 1 satisfying it somewhat, and 0 not satisfying it at all.

As you fill out your chart, you may find that you have some holes or just don't know how to rank a school in terms of a certain characteristic. This could mean you need to do some more research. Or it may be that this particular area is no longer that important to you.

Even if a college scores high overall but has a quality you know you can't stand, it probably shouldn't make it on your final list. Likewise, if there is something you can't live without, colleges lacking that quality aren't those where you should apply. Be reasonable and realistic when considering what you can and can't live without, but know that this is a great way to prioritize.

> *"As time went on, eliminating schools became easier. During my junior year I realized that I loved French more than anything else I studied. I started eliminating schools that didn't have French as an available major."*
>
> **Freshman,**
> **Fairfield University**

This ranking exercise might seem cumbersome at first, but it can really be a life saver in helping you organize your thoughts, research, and impressions into something that helps you make a decision. Just remember that there's no science to this process—it's a step to help you prioritize your choices and consider each college in comparison to the others. At the end of the day trust your gut feelings and if a college just feels right, it's probably a great place for you to go.

COMPARE AND CONTRAST COLLEGES TEMPLATE

Name of College	College 1	College 2	College 3	College 4	College 5	College 6	College 7	College 8
Academically challenging	3	2	2	2	1	1	3	3
Good English dept.	2	1	2	2	2	1	2	1
Good Spanish dept.	1	1	2	1	3	2	2	3
Medium-sized school	3	1	0	2	2	2	3	3
Ethnically diverse student body	1	3	1	1	2	3	2	3
Located in the Northeast	3	0	3	3	0	3	3	1
Urban or college town environment	0	3	3	3	0	3	2	2
Able to study abroad	0	0	1	2	3	0	1	2
Theater club	2	0	2	1	3	0	1	2
Able to join social activist group	1	2	3	2	1	3	3	3
TOTAL	**16**	**13**	**19**	**19**	**17**	**18**	**22**	**23**

DIVERSIFY YOUR CHOICES

One of the most important things you should do while deciding where to apply is to diversify your college choices based on the difficulty of getting in and overall cost of attendance. Even if you have every bit of confidence in your ability to get into a top school and get enough financial aid and scholarships to pay for it, you have to have a Plan B, and it should be a Plan B with which you can be happy. You may never have to go to Plan B, but you'll feel more confident and secure if you know that you're okay if for whatever reason you can't get into your "reach" or ideal school.

> *"I think the most important thing is to really like your safeties. I loved my safety, and I got into it first, so it took a lot of pressure off all the other schools. I have a lot of friends who ended up at their safeties, which they didn't like and they're sort of unhappy there."*

> **Junior,**
> **Harvard University**

You can call them whatever you like, but make sure that you apply to some reach, medium difficulty, and safety schools in terms of difficulty of acceptance.

- A **reach** school is one where your chance of admittance is not likely, but not outside the realm of possibility (25% chance or less).

- A **medium difficulty** school is one where you're pretty sure you can get in (let's call it a 75% chance).

- A **safety** is one where your chance of admittance is pretty much a sure thing (90-100%).

Now that you have the categories, how do you spread out the odds? There's no science to this and no magic formula, but based on our interviews with students and checking with admissions counselors, here's a ratio you can start with:

Let's say you're applying to between six and eight schools. The bulk of them—about three or four—should fall in the medium difficulty category. One or two should be reaches. You don't want to be rejected from every school you apply to, but at the same time it's good to shoot high with a couple, because hey, you never know. And definitely select one or two safeties to fall back on. Just keep in mind that you could end up going to one of them, so make sure you like them enough to live with that if it happens.

> *"I didn't apply to some super-competitive schools, but I wish I had. In retrospect, I might've gotten in, but I got intimidated and didn't leave myself the opportunity. I loved where I ended up going, but my advice would be to not sell yourself short and apply to several reach schools, even if they seem intimidating."*
>
> **Recent Grad,**
> **Wesleyan University**

As you go through and categorize your college selections, think about cost. Unless you're in the lucky situation of not having to worry about paying for college, this is an important factor. Don't ever rule out a school just because it's expensive—your family likely qualifies for financial aid and you can get scholarships and grants to make up the difference between the cost and what your family can pay.

At the same time, it's important to have a financial safety school on your list—just in case.

THINK ABOUT EARLY DECISION

"My big mistake was deciding where I was going to apply Early Decision before I'd looked at any of the schools. I ended up not applying early to my number one choice school and applying early, I'm told, might have been that one extra thing that would've gotten me in."

Freshman,
Harvard University

If you have a very clear first choice that you feel is a perfect fit for you, Early Decision can be the right way to go. This is how it works:

You get to apply early to the school of your dreams—in most cases, your application has to be in by November 15th. You also get to hear back early, by mid-December, whether you've been accepted, rejected, or deferred to regular decision. Here's the tricky part: By applying Early Decision, you're agreeing in advance to attend that school if you're accepted and you can only apply to one school using this method. You're allowed to apply to other schools under regular application procedures, but if you're accepted by your Early Decision school you must then withdraw your applications from all other colleges.

"I applied Early Decision to Vassar. It was definitely my number one choice. I really wanted to show them that I was 100% interested, so I filled out the

Vassar application instead of the common one. I didn't have the best SATs, but I had really good grades and a lot of extracurriculars. When I got accepted, it just confirmed that it was the right place for me to go. It was nice to be able to take a deep sigh and enjoy my senior year."

**Recent Grad,
Vassar College**

According to the College Board, about a quarter of all four-year colleges have some sort of early application program and about 14% of college applicants go this route. The College Board's Web site, **www.CollegeBoard.org**, has a list of colleges that offer either Early Decision or Early Action. There are stats on the number of students who applied this way and were accepted—check it out.

There has been a lot of controversy in recent years about the fairness or lack or fairness of the Early Decision system. Similarly, there are never-ending arguments about just how much better your chances of admission are if you apply early—they are better, but how much better? We're not experts on this and won't go into detail here, but you should discuss this option with your parents and your guidance counselor. Applying Early Decision is a significant commitment.

Many colleges now offer Early Action as an option to applicants. Under this procedure, you apply early, like you do for Early Decision, but if you're accepted at a school, you're not obligated to go there. If you like a certain college but aren't one hundred percent sure that you want to enroll, or need to see what your financial aid packages come out to be, this option might be a good choice for you.

EARLY DECISION PROS AND CONS

PROS	CONS
Relief to know early where you're going to college	Can't change your mind if you're accepted
Increases chances of admission for many students	Risk not getting enough financial aid or scholarships
Takes pressure off senior year	Have less time to research schools and apply
Saves money on application costs	Your senior-year achievements can't strengthen your application

"I'm much more willing to take a risk on a candidate who has made a commitment to us by applying Early Decision. With Early Action or Regular Decision we don't know if we're your first or eighth choice and we simply don't have enough spots for all of the qualified students. If you apply Early Decision, we're going to try to help you out if we think that you can do the work. This guarantees nothing, of course, but gives you some insight into our philosophy on this topic."

**Dean of Admissions,
Babson College**

GET FEEDBACK

Deciding where to apply to college is a big decision and you shouldn't make big decisions without talking them over with other knowledgeable people. Definitely get feedback on your choices from your parents, guidance counselors, or college advisors (if your school has them). Tell them where you're thinking of applying and ask for their opinions and feedback.

Listen to what your trusted resources have to say. You may agree with them, or you may not. Take it all in and decide what is useful or relevant. Keep an open mind but remember—this is your decision.

"My dad advised me to go to Columbia. I think he felt that the kinds of opportunities I would have there would be pretty tremendous and would be worth the money. Easy for him to say. But in the end, it really was. I think that parents want you to go where you're going to be happy, but I think a lot of them are also enticed by the pull of a big name university."

**Recent Grad,
Columbia University**

9

conquer
standardized
tests

Standardized tests, and particularly the SAT I, are a source of a lot of anxiety for most of us. It's a lot of pressure to study and do well because admissions committees do take the results into account. What's important to remember is that standardized test scores are never the sole or most important factor that will determine your acceptance or rejection from a certain school. Instead, these scores are considered as another data point about your qualifications, and if they aren't great, you can make it up with stellar grades or strong and eclectic extracurricular involvement.

In this chapter we've put together our suggestions for how to increase your chances of doing your best on the SAT I and other standardized tests you might be required to take.

KNOW WHAT TESTS YOU NEED
▼
PLAN AHEAD
▼
GET SOME HELP
▼
PRACTICE, PRACTICE, PRACTICE
▼
DO IT AGAIN...IF YOU NEED TO
▼
KEEP THINGS IN PERSPECTIVE

KNOW WHAT TESTS YOU NEED

Almost all colleges and universities will require you to take either the Scholastic Aptitude Test (SAT I) or the American College Testing Assessment (ACT). Both the SAT I and ACT test a combination of math and verbal skills. Even if the schools in which you're most interested do not require SAT I scores, we recommend that you take them anyway. You might need them if you change your mind and want to apply somewhere else.

Many colleges also require you to take at least three SAT II tests in addition to the SAT I or the ACT. These tests are subject-specific, testing everything from advanced math to writing and history. While some schools will require that you take certain SAT II tests, others will only indicate how many you should take and leave the subjects up to you. For instance, most schools require that you take the SAT II Writing test and at least one out of a number of SAT II math tests. Make sure to know the requirements of every college where you're applying.

Another type of common standardized tests is the Advanced Placement (AP) exam. These tests are also subject-specific, and they're derived from the curriculum of AP classes offered at your high school. AP tests aren't required for college admission, but if you're in an AP class and are doing well, consider taking the test. Even if you don't get a 5—the highest score on an AP test—taking these very tough tests shows that you're an ambitious and serious student. In addition, most colleges will give you course credit for certain AP tests and you might be able to avoid taking placement exams for some college courses.

On the next page is a brief summary of the SAT I, SAT II, and ACT tests, which will give you a quick idea about their similarities and differences.

STANDARDIZED TESTS COMPARISON

TEST	DESCRIPTION	WHEN TO TAKE
SAT I	• Three-hour exam that measures verbal and math skills. • Maximum score on each section is 800, for a total of 1,600.	Usually taken for the first time during the spring of junior year and repeated, if necessary, during the fall of senior year.
ACT	• Three-hour exam that measures achievement in English, Math, Reading, and Science. • Scores on each section are averaged to create a composite score. Maximum score is 36.	Same as the SAT I.
SAT II	• One-hour exams that measure mastery of a particular field of study such as Math, Writing, or Science. • 22 subject tests are currently offered. • Maximum score is 800.	The best time to take a SAT II test is soon after you've finished studying that particular subject in school.

PLAN AHEAD

The SAT I and the ACT are the most important tests for your college application. Most college-bound students take one of these exams during the spring of their junior year and we suggest that you do this as well. There are a few advantages to taking these tests early:

- You'll have plenty of time to study and re-take the test if you don't like your scores the first time around.

- The SAT I and the ACT are offered much more frequently in the spring than the fall, leaving you with many more opportunities to fit them into your schedule.

- You want to take the SAT I or the ACT by the time you send in your application, and if you're applying Early Decision or Early Action to any colleges, many of the fall test dates might be too late.

- If you get your standardized tests out of the way by your senior year you'll have more time—and less stress—to focus on writing your college essays and filling out applications. And less stress is definitely a great thing.

GET SOME HELP

SAT I and ACT scores are important and you want to make sure that you do your best. A lot of it has to do with your general knowledge of the subject matter but a great deal depends on how well you're prepared to take these particular tests. Sure, we've all taken tests in high school, but these are different, and as smart as you might be, you need to study for them.

There are many helpful resources out there to help you get ready for standardized tests. Below is a quick rundown of the most common study aids, courses, and materials. Research a few, consider your resources, but our main advice is that you do take the time to study and get some help doing it.

▶FREE STUFF

Your guidance counselor's office should have copies of *Taking the SAT I,* which includes tips on taking the test as well as a sample test with answers. There's also a publication called *Taking the SAT II,* which describes the format of the tests and has a few sample questions.

Several websites, like **www.CollegeBoard.org**, also offer free practice tests.

▶BOOKS

There are whole aisles in bookstores dedicated to standardized test prep books. Make sure that whatever book you get has several practice tests and is recently published so you get the latest information. Many books now come with a CD-ROM that contains one or more of the practice tests—we definitely recommend that you take advantage of this option.

You should choose whatever book you think will help you study, but our favorite is 10 Real SATs, published by The College Board. This is the only book that has 10 real SAT I tests that are actual tests from previous years. There's nothing like taking an actual test to prepare.

▶PREP COURSES

Prep courses are usually taught during a 10-week period and cost somewhere between $400 and $1,000. The two most popular companies that offer standardized test classes are Princeton Review and Kaplan, but there are many smaller local companies as well.

There are several advantages to taking a test prep course. Perhaps the biggest one is that a course will force you to study for your test by assigning homework and involving you in classroom activities. Not only will you be working hard, you will be working hard in the right ways: doing exercises and learning valuable test-taking skills. Getting used to the format of the specific test questions, learning how to time yourself, how to attack each question and guess strategically—these are all very important to your success and these are the skills that are at the core of the test prep courses.

The major disadvantage to taking prep courses is money—they are expensive. If you can't afford the high price tag, don't despair. Many students do very well on these tests without taking a class. Get a book or two, take many practice tests, and you'll be well prepared.

If you do take a test prep course, make sure to invest the required time into it. Go to class, do your homework, and take practice tests. There's no magic bullet, and if you don't practice, no course will increase your score.

Online test prep courses are becoming more popular, so look into this option if you'd like a structured preparation curriculum but don't have the time to go to actual classes. Online classes range in price from $300 to $700.

▶PRIVATE TUTOR

You can also hire a private tutor to help you prepare for the standardized tests. The major advantage of this choice is that you'll receive one-on-one instruction entirely concentrated on you and geared towards only your requirements. You can focus on the types of questions where you need the most help and customize the course of study to your specific needs.

"I had a one-on-one tutor for the SAT I and I actually did improve my score significantly. We went over specific parts of the tests and reviewed vocabulary, which was really useful. Because it was just me and the tutor, we were able to go over my specific areas of confusion, and I didn't have to sit in a class going over stuff I already understood."

**Sophomore,
Skidmore College**

Hiring a private tutor is often even more expensive than taking a prep course. Also, you risk hiring someone who isn't great at what they do or not extremely well qualified. Make sure to do your research, understand why the person is qualified to help you increase your score, and always, always ask for references.

> "I felt a lot of pressure to hire an SAT tutor so I hired a guy, thinking that I was going to get really good help. Well, I had one or two sessions with him and he ran off with my money. I was totally scammed. I ended up increasing my score by 200 points, but it had nothing to do with a tutor. Instead, I'd say buy the book called 10 Real SATs and practice a lot."

> **Senior,**
> **University of Pennsylvania**

PRACTICE, PRACTICE, PRACTICE

We asked dozens of our friends and fellow college students about what helped them do well on the SAT I and the ACT and it's no surprise that we got one answer over and over: PRACTICE. A lot of what goes into a good standardized test score is being familiar with the format of the test and being used to the specific way in which each type of question is asked. The more you practice, the more comfortable you become with the test and the more likely you'll be to focus, think clearly, and avoid getting too stressed out.

As you practice for the tests, it's a good idea to first focus on getting the right answers and then make sure that you can complete the test in the specified amount of time. Work through the problems, check your answers, figure out why you got a question right or wrong, and don't worry about the time limit too much. You need to develop a strategy for answering each question and it's best to work it out without the pressure of time. Once you feel more comfortable and have your approach, work on timing yourself to make sure that you get through the entire test.

You don't have endless hours of free time to practice so it's a good idea to prioritize what you'll study and practice most vigorously. If verbal questions are your strength, spend more time on the math section and vice versa. If a certain type of question—such as reading comprehension— gives you the most trouble, spend more time practicing those sections than others. You know what you need to improve, so create a plan for study and focus on those areas where you need the most work.

Definitely take at least two or three full-length practice tests before you go in for the real thing. Follow the rules— time yourself and take the test in a quiet space and during the same time of day when you'd be taking the real test. The closer you can make your experience to the real one, the better prepared you'll be.

DO IT AGAIN...IF YOU NEED TO

You might do great on your first try. But if your score is not as high as you'd like, take the test again. See what you need to improve, work on more practice questions in that section, and go into your second shot with the confidence that you've done this before and can do it again and do it better.

The scores from every SAT I and ACT test that you take will be reported to the colleges that you indicate on your registration form. So if you take the test twice, two scores will be reported. Colleges differ in terms of how they treat multiple scores—some average your scores, some use only your latest score or your highest. Many students take the test at least a few times, so there's nothing wrong with that and you won't be penalized if you repeat the SAT I or the ACT.

You don't have too much to lose by repeating these tests. You have a shot at improving your score and a low risk of doing much worse than you did the first time around. And you're definitely demonstrating to the admissions committee that you're a hard worker and are trying to do as well as you can by taking the test again.

KEEP THINGS IN PERSPECTIVE

It's pretty easy to get caught up with your standardized test scores and obsess about doing well. But if you make yourself overly anxious about the outcome you'll be stressed out when taking the test and won't be able to concentrate as well as you should.

> *"Although SATs are extremely intimidating—they terrified me!—I've realized that stressing out about them is really a waste of time. It worries you and definitely doesn't improve your chances of getting a higher score. My advice is to try and approach this test with confidence and stay calm. This will help you avoid freaking out or going blank, which does happen if you stress out too much."*
>
> **Freshman,**
> **Fordham University**

Instead of stressing out, remember that you've learned a lot in high school and have taken the time to practice and prepare—you're capable of translating all that work into a good score. Besides, standardized test scores are just one component of what the admissions people will look at when considering your application. Not doing well on these tests doesn't automatically mean that you won't get into the college of your choice, so try not to drive yourself crazy over them.

Megan's corner
▼

This might sound obvious, but try to avoid talking about scores with your friends. My whole grade talked about them way too much and I definitely ended up offending some people, and some people offended me, often unintentionally. Don't fall into the trap of comparing yourself to other people. Not only will this make you feel better, but you'll avoid unnecessary tension.

▲

10

ace your applications

The prospect of actually filling out your college applications can be daunting. These few pieces of paper, together with your essays, recommendations, grades, and test scores are what some mysterious admissions committees will use to figure out if they'd like to see you enrolled in their school. Somehow you've got to come alive as a person through these papers, and that's the task that we found the toughest during this process.

You can do it, though. In this chapter we've collected suggestions on how to go about filling out your applications and making yourself stand out as a great candidate. If you get organized and leave yourself enough time, you might even enjoy this part of the college application process.

TAKE CARE OF THE LOGISTICS
▼
LEAVE YOURSELF ENOUGH TIME
▼
CREATE A DRAFT APPPLICATION
▼
DO THE EASY STUFF FIRST
▼
HYPE UP YOUR ACHIEVEMENTS
▼
DRAFT PARAGRAPH RESPONSES
▼
MAKE IT LOOK GOOD
▼
AVOID UNNECESSARY SUPPLEMENTS

TAKE CARE OF THE LOGISTICS

"I had fun with the actual applications—filling them all out, answering the stupid "Why do like ___?" questions. I figured, here's my chance to show what I have, and show the enthusiasm and excitement I have about potentially going to Brown."

**Sophomore,
Brown University**

First thing's first: To apply, you need an application. Most colleges and universities make their applications available sometime in mid-summer, and you should try to get those applications in your hands as soon as possible. To get a hard copy of a school's application, you can call up the admissions office or go to their website. Many colleges let you fill out their application online, and some even waive the application fees if you do this. Take advantage of this option if you feel comfortable—it will make your application look neat and you'll avoid the all-dreaded, lost-in-the-mail scenario.

Megan's corner
▼

I found the Internet absolutely invaluable in getting and filing applications. I would say the safest way to make sure you have all the necessary materials is to request a hard, paper copy of the application from the college (by calling, mailing, or e-mailing the admissions office), but then doing the actual application online, if that option is available. Personally, it helped my focus and thinking process to have a printed copy in front of me to scratch down notes before I filled out the online application.

▲

More than 230 colleges and universities in the U.S. accept the Common Application, which was designed to simplify the application process: You fill it out once and send copies of it to colleges that accept it. If you're applying to a school that does, take advantage of this option. You might worry that filling out the Common Application is too generic and doesn't show the school that you're interested in it, but we've talked to many admissions officers and that's definitely not the case. You can get copies of the Common Application in your guidance counselor's office, or online at **www.CommonApplication.org**.

Once you start receiving applications in the mail (or once you start printing out copies for yourself from the Internet), the amount of paper alone can make it hard to keep track of everything. Try to stick to the filing system we talked about at the beginning of this book and as applications arrive, put them in the folder dedicated to that particular school. Also make sure to mark on your calendar the date when you have to send in each of your applications.

> *"Try not to work on more than three applications at a time—any more than that and you'll increase your chances of making a silly mistake on one of them. The admissions officer at Yale will definitely not like to see that you sent in your essay in which you talk about the beautiful Stanford campus."*

> **Freshman,**
> **Emory University**

Each college's application form will have a checklist of tasks you must perform to produce a completed application. Place this checklist at the front of your folder and remember to check off the tasks as you complete them. By sticking to a checklist, you can keep a close eye on your progress with each application and avoid getting confused when you're working on several of them.

LEAVE YOURSELF ENOUGH TIME

> *"Everyone told me to work on my applications during the summer, but I didn't and screwed myself by forcing myself to write applications during the usual school, sports, and craziness of the fall."*
>
> **Recent Grad,**
> **Princeton University**

Try to get started with your applications during the summer before your senior year. You'll be able to get organized before the hustle and bustle of classes and activities begins and will feel like you're in control of this process. If you're applying Early Decision or Early Action, starting early is even more important.

You might be applying to some schools that use Rolling Admissions. This means that they will accept and evaluate applications as they come in. This is different from the regular admissions procedure where the admissions committee waits until all applications are in before beginning the evaluation process. If you're applying to a school with Rolling Admissions, get your application in as soon as possible, and definitely don't wait until the days close to the deadline, as many spots will have been taken.

"The key to college admissions is to be prompt. A lot of bigger schools, like the University of Central Florida, have Rolling Admissions, and the sooner you get your application in, the sooner you hear from them. I applied to UCF in early September and by Halloween, I was set for the next four years. It made the rest of high school much more enjoyable for me because the stress of applications was long out of the way."

Sophomore,
University of Central Florida

CREATE A DRAFT APPLICATION

Before you dive into filling out the applications for each school, you might find it useful to create a master draft application. It will have the basic information that you need so you won't have to go hunting for it and you'll have practiced writing about your achievements to make them stand out as much as possible.

The Common App works really well for this purpose. Take a copy of it and fill it out as completely as you can—the basic personal information about you and your parents, your grades and scores, as well as information about your extracurricular activities and jobs. Try to do it as thoroughly and completely as possible, as if this were the real thing.

After you've filled out your draft application, take some time to look it over and see if there's any information that you need to research and get—such as your parents' highest educational degree—or anything that you need to re-write to make it sound stronger and more unique. In a few sections we'll talk about making the most out of your achievements and you should make sure that they come out as strong as possible on your draft application.

DO THE EASY STUFF FIRST

We suggest that you start by filling out the objective, fill-in-the-blank sections at the beginning of each college application. These sections ask for your name, address, secondary school information, family background, citizenship, standardized test scores, and so on. By getting this part done first you'll feel accomplished and in control of your application. Use your draft application as you work through these sections to ensure that you're including the correct information.

Take care in filling out these sections—they seem simple enough, but you'll probably never be as unsure of your own middle name as when you're sitting there poised to write it in on a college application.

WE TALK WITH...

Arar Han
Senior, Boston College

Did you have a plan for how to approach your college applications?

I realized that my four years of high school were all related to my college applications. So I drew up a plan early on, making sure I scheduled my SAT II exams to coordinate with my course schedule—for instance, making sure I took the Chemistry SAT II the June of my sophomore year, when I took chemistry honors. I also realized that I could get better recommendations if I got to know the teachers I liked best outside of regular coursework. Not that people ought to brown-nose their teachers around town—that would be singularly annoying from the point of view of the teacher—but if I liked the teacher and thought that she or he would be the one writing my recommendation, I would make sure I went to review sessions and chatted with them during breaks on various topics of common interest.

Do you think your plan was successful? What would you change if you could do it again?

My plan was successful in that I had a very well-rounded application. But I think that I would not be so concerned about the application if I had to do it over again. I didn't really know how to just kick back and be a high school kid. Thinking about my college apps early on helped me get a good application, but I wonder what I lost by obsessing about standardized test scores and trying to be so well-rounded.

HYPE UP YOUR ACHIEVEMENTS

The objective part of your applications will often ask you to list extracurricular activities, jobs, what you did on your summer vacation, and so on. These sections seem as simple as filling out your address, but they are actually a great opportunity for you to demonstrate your accomplishments to admissions officers even before your essays. And while your activities and jobs at this point are what they are, you can make them sound great and strong through the way that you write about them.

> *"You have to remember that the admissions officers are people, too, and they want to see people. They want to read about real lives, not high schoolers serving up their life achievements glazed over in glitter."*

**Sophomore,
Brown University**

The basic thing to remember is that your achievements only speak as loudly as you present them. If you're captain of the basketball team, don't just list "Varsity Basketball" in the activities section—make sure you mention your rank as captain and the length of time that you've held this position. If you are the treasurer of the honor society or the bookkeeper of your school newspaper, include those roles as part of your descriptions.

Colleges are not only looking for your participation in extracurricular activities. They are also looking for the level of your involvement and leadership. Think quality over quantity. List those activities where you've had a leadership role first. For example, if you're President of the senior class, you should list that before citing your membership on the backgammon team during freshman year. If you're captain of the soccer team, you should list that before your membership on student council. And don't be modest— make sure that the admissions committee knows that you were a first-team all-county selection for tennis, or that your mock trial team went to the state finals.

Your application will also include a section asking for your employment record. If you're like many of us, you've probably had a few part-time jobs, and although they might not seem that special to you, include them on your application. A record of employment demonstrates that you can manage your busy life as a student as well as your job responsibilities. It shows that you're responsible and hardworking, and these are great qualities.

As with your extracurriculars, make sure to list your most impressive jobs or internships first. You should also be clear and describe the duties you performed at your job. Certain job titles—such as "cashier" or "sales representative"—are pretty self-explanatory. Others need a more detailed explanation. For instance, the job title "office assistant" is extremely vague. As an office assistant, your responsibilities would range from getting coffee and licking stamps to doing Internet research, designing community service projects, and anything in between. For these vague job titles, be sure to elaborate on your responsibilities. The employment section is not simply asking whether or not you've had a job, but also asking what you've done.

Besides extracurriculars and jobs, you should include in the achievements section of your application any academic or other awards you've received. Be specific and include descriptions for awards that aren't commonly known. Everyone knows what the National Merit Scholarship is, but your Jane McCormick Scholarship from sophomore year requires some explanation.

WE TALK WITH...

Owen Whitehurst
Freshman, Emory University

What were some things that you wish you'd done differently when applying to college?

I should've started earlier on getting letters of recommendation. The mad dash for letters right before applications were due was extremely stressful, both for me and the teachers writing the letters. Getting a head start on that would've been very beneficial to my application process.

What was the best piece of advice you got about applying/getting into college, and who gave it to you?

In high school I was active in student government. My guidance counselor told me to really emphasize what I'd done through student government on my college applications, and I really feel like that is one of the major reasons that I got into Emory. Everyone who is applying to good schools has good grades and most likely a lot of strong extracurricular activities. What I think made me unique was that I chose one extracurricular activity and really delved into what I accomplished through it.

What was the worst piece of advice you received and from whom?

The worst piece of advice I received was when a few parents of friends who were already in college told me to hire a private college counselor. Quite honestly I have ended up fine without one, and I can say that my college application essays were truly my own.

DRAFT PARAGRAPH RESPONSES

In addition to the long essays or personal statements, about which we talk in a separate chapter, most college applications will include several shorter essays, usually in the section with extracurricular activities. For example, you might be asked to write a few paragraphs about an extracurricular activity that has meant the most to you or from which you've learned something valuable.

Make sure to draft your response to these questions separately and treat them seriously as you would your longer essays. Admissions officers do read them, and if written with care, they can enhance your application. It's another way to bring you and what you've done to life, and that's what you're after in a great college application.

MAKE IT LOOK GOOD

You're putting a tremendous amount of work into your college applications and essays and you want to make sure that they look as great and neat as possible when you send them in. Here are a few suggestions:

✓ **Type or fill out your application online, if possible**. A typed application looks neat and is easier to read. It shows that you went that one extra step to present yourself in the most professional way, and that's another point in your favor.

✓ **Proofread every section**. You might think that you know how to write or type out your address by now, but check it over anyway. Careless mistakes show that you didn't put enough effort and attention into your application. They are also distracting to the reader.

✓ **Ask someone else to proofread your application.** You've been looking at the same information day after day and may miss a thing or two. Ask your parents, your siblings, or your guidance counselor to proofread your applications before you send them out. A fresh set of eyes can really help.

✓ **Check your checklist.** Go over the checklist that came with every application and make sure that you've included every piece of paper and information, including your application fee.

✓ **Make a copy of your application.** Things happen and you never know when your application might get lost in the mail (knock on wood!). Make a copy to have as backup.

WORST CASE SCENARIO

by
Emily Newman
Senior, University of Pennsylvania

It was a dark and stormy Halloween night and I was inside my house in front of my computer typing up my college application. November 1st was the big deadline for my application for my first choice college—it was do or die. Of course I had procrastinated and put it off until the last minute. I had two essays to do, but I had put so much time and effort into one of them that I had completely forgotten about the other. Way to go me. While all my friends were out partying their senior-year Halloween away, I got to hang out with my mom.

As I'm finally making some progress, the doorbell rings. It's my little neighbor, so of course my mom and I go out to compliment her costume. Then, I attempt to open the door and we have successfully locked ourselves out of our own house. Panic quickly sets in as time ticks away before the post office will close its doors as well as my door to the future! My great idea is to just knock down the door, but my mom would rather not. After fighting for a bit, I finally open the door. Ha! I am now a genius and my mom loves me again.

But there's more. I finally finish the stupid application and can begin to breathe again. My mom begins looking over it and with one little knock of her hand, her glass of water tips over onto my application! More panic!!! How can I send in a wet application? Nobody wants a watermarked application no matter how high the SATs! I'm now there with my mom, very unhappy, while she is holding the application, being careful not to smudge it, and I am holding the hairdryer. Is this a Halloween party or what? Finally my somewhat moist application was sent in and on time. The moral of the story is: Be thrifty and clever when in such a bind. Do not put off your key to the future until the future, because sooner rather than later the future will knock on your door, and then lock you outside of it, without even a hairdryer to save you.

AVOID UNNECESSARY SUPPLEMENTS

You've probably heard a story or two about students sending in photographs, videotapes, and voice recordings with their applications. And if you've seen the movie "Legally Blonde" you might think that supplements like that can work as well for you as they did for Elle in helping her get into Harvard Law School. But movies are fantasies and from what we've been able to gather from fellow students and admissions officers, you're better off sending in only what's required.

Sure, you do a great handstand and can sing like Pavarotti, but unless you're applying to a performing arts school, keep these talents to yourself. Admissions committees rarely look at videos, and including something like that can distract them from the core of your application and can hurt your chances.

Megan's corner
▼

In one of the many college presentations I went to junior and senior year, an admissions officer told us about a kid who, for his essay, had written a play and had included hand puppets with which to act it out. It caught their attention for sure, but the admissions officers didn't have time to act it out and it ended up being more distracting than helpful.

▲

If you're applying to a school where you have to present some kind of a portfolio—photographs, drawings, etc.—make sure to find out exactly what you need to submit. These requirements should be listed on the application, but if not, call up the school and find out.

WE TALK WITH...

Michael Gallant
Senior, Columbia University

Did you have a plan for how to approach your college applications?

I wanted to present myself as honestly as possible. I felt like it would be a bad idea to try to transform myself into "the perfect candidate" when I don't really think such a thing exists. If a school wasn't going to take me for who I really was, it probably wouldn't be the best place for me anyway.

Do you think your plan was successful?

I was happy with the results of my applications. I got my share of rejections, but I was also lucky enough to have some good choices in front of me. Looking back on four crazy, amazing years at Columbia, I can say that the decision to come to New York was a good one.

What was the most difficult part of the application process?

Waiting. After putting in all that effort, I wanted instant answers.

What would you say to high juniors and seniors as they try to tackle their college apps?

Try to find the place that's best for you, regardless of name or prestige. Being happy for four years of your life is infinitely more important than a name on a diploma. Also, try to keep a sense of perspective: One thick or thin envelope will not make or break your life. Really. Just be chill, do your best, and see what happens.

11

write
memorable
essays

Essays are a critical part of your college application because they give you the opportunity to tell the admissions officers about who you are and what matters to you, and do this in your own words. Winning essays have the power to overshadow your grades and less-than-stellar SAT scores.

Because they matter so much, essays are a source of great anxiety for all of us. It's daunting to think that you have to make a personal impression on the admission committee in a few written paragraphs. We won't deny that writing essays will be a stressful experience, but if you leave yourself enough time to go through several drafts and write about something important to you, you can create a really impressive essay.

ANSWER THE QUESTION
▼
BE YOURSELF AND SHOW YOUR PASSION
▼
DON'T WHINE
▼
RE-WRITE YOUR INTRODUCTION
▼
REVISE CONTENT AND WRITING
▼
GET FEEDBACK AND ADVICE
▼
AVOID COMMON TRAPS
▼
PROOFREAD LIKE A MANIAC

ANSWER THE QUESTION

Some applications ask you to choose from a list of topics for your essays while others leave it completely up to you. Here are some common examples:

- "Evaluate a significant experience, achievement, or risk you have taken, or an ethical dilemma you have faced and its impact on you."

- "Discuss some issue of personal, local, national, or international concern and its importance to you."

- "Indicate a person who has had a significant influence on you, and describe that influence."

- "Describe a character in fiction, an historical figure, or a creative work (as in art, music, science, etc.), that has had an influence on you, and explain that influence."

- "Topic of your choice."

Whichever topic you choose, make sure that your essay actually addresses that topic and answers the question(s) posed. Essay topics are usually very broad and allow you a lot of wiggle room for creativity—we know students who responded to the question about meaningful life experiences with everything from community service to getting arrested. But you should address the broad topic in the core of your essay—if you're writing about a person who has influenced you, don't spend most of your essay talking about the value of world peace in your life.

"Some schools have gone to a wonderful system of 'invent your own question.' The rationale is that the question you choose is often as revealing about your personality as the answer you give. I personally

loved that because it allowed me to write one less essay, or it allowed me to write an essay about a subject that really moved me."

**Freshman,
Princeton University**

The trick to writing an effective essay is to create a specific and meaningful answer to a very broad topic question. If you're writing about a meaningful experience in your life, be very specific about WHAT the experience entailed, WHY it was meaningful, and HOW it impacted your life.

For example, say you're writing about your first significant leadership experience—becoming the President of your high school debate club—and you want to express how daunting it was to be in charge of a group of people who looked up to you.

Here's a very general way to describe how this experience affected you:

> *"It was a really difficult and intimidating time for me."*

You could've written this sentence about anything. It's not specific and it does not say WHY the experience was so difficult.

Here's a better way to express the same point:

> *"For the first time in my life I was responsible for leading a group of people who relied on me for direction, major decisions, and, the scariest of all, achieving our goal."*

As you begin to brainstorm and get ready to write your essays, you might find it helpful to do a quick what, how, and why check of your topic. We also suggest that you do this after you write your essay: Put yourself into the reader's shoes and see if this essay tells you what the particular experience/influence was, how it impacted the writer's life, and why it was an important impact.

✓ **WHAT**: What happened, what is the specific experience about which you're writing.

✓ **HOW**: How did what happened influence you, how did it impact your life, and how did you grow as a person.

✓ **WHY**: Why was this experience meaningful or important, why was this person a significant influence on your life, why do you care about what happened.

☞ RECYCLING ESSAYS—DO OR DON'T?

You've probably heard the phrase "recycling essays" before—it refers to using the same essay for several college applications. If you could do this, your life would certainly be easier and there are some experts out there that claim to teach you how to do this. We're not those experts, but we've talked to some admissions counselors and dozens of students and here's what we think:

If you're applying to two colleges that have the same question or topic for your essays, there's absolutely nothing wrong in sending the same essay to both. The respective admissions committees aren't going to call each other up and compare notes on what essay you sent to each. So if two colleges ask that you write about a meaningful experience that affected your life, you can send your essay about traveling to Nigeria to both of them.

What we don't recommend is that you use the same or very similar essay for two different topics. For example, let's say the topic asks you about what advice you'd give to your fellow high school graduates. If you write "I'd advise my fellow graduates to always be strong," and then proceed to copy the essay you wrote about your friend dying in a motorcycle accident, you won't fool anyone. Recycled essays are extremely easy to spot and you'd be jeopardizing your chances of acceptance if you reuse essays indiscriminately.

SHOW WHAT YOU'LL BRING

by
Cicely Ott
Sophomore, Middlebury College

Despite the fact that many people seem to dread the essay portion of college applications, I have to say that it was my favorite part. By the time you apply to college, there isn't much left to be done about three years' worth of grades, about how time out of class has been spent, or about what various teachers think of you. The essay part of the application is basically the only thing over which you still have a lot of control and it's your chance to give the admissions folks an idea of who you really are.

I remember trying to think of something to say that would give readers a window into *me*, and it was the best feeling to realize that I wasn't trying to prove anything in my essay. As far as I can tell, there's little to be done at this point about whether or not you are the right caliber student for a particular institution. But, once a person's grades and other past performances show that he or she is an academically qualified applicant, it's all about the essay. Use your essay to show readers something amazing about you—show your school of choice that you have something special to bring to its community.

BE YOURSELF AND SHOW YOUR PASSION

There's no right answer to the essay questions. You don't have to write about wanting to change the world—in fact, this is too broad and too clichéd a topic. What you do have to write about is something that's meaningful to you and has somehow affected your life.

Some people's lives are filled with tremendous difficulties or exciting events, others' aren't. You shouldn't feel that just because you didn't live in a foreign country when you were twelve or had someone important in your life die that you don't have anything significant to write about. Any experience that was meaningful to you can tell a personal story to the admissions committee—as long as you describe what it was, why it was important, and how it impacted your life. In fact, sometimes essays about pretty common experiences that have an unexpected impact on your life can be much more memorable than those about tremendous experiences that have a predictable impact.

> *"My family immigrated to the U.S. when I was thirteen and I was going to write at least some of my essays about the difficulties we encountered in trying to re-start our lives in a different country. My friends were jealous that I had such a unique topic, but I struggled with it—everything I wrote sounded like such a cliché."*
>
> **Recent Grad,
> Wesleyan University**

Care about what you're writing and let your passion come through. Avoid being too over the top, but this is not the time to tone down your emotions. You have one shot to impress your unique personality on the admissions committee—do it on your essay!

> *"One of my career goals is to become a Supreme Court Justice. For my college essay, I wrote my memoirs as if I was a Supreme Court Justice and I talked about the issues that are important to me. My advice is to take some aspect of your life that is unique and shape an essay around it."*
>
> **Freshman,**
> **Emory University**

"Be yourself in completing your college application. Don't be tempted to tell us what you think we want to hear, but let us hear what is important to you—your likes, dislikes, priorities, and passions. In this way we can evaluate how you will contribute to the college."

**Dean of Admissions,
University of Pennsylvania**

IT'S ALL ABOUT PASSION

by
Sher Kung
Sophomore, Brown University

Sure, you need to be a competent writer, but I strongly feel that you just have to express yourself passionately in order to compose a convincing and stand-out essay. I write a lot in my spare time—the material in my journal was probably ten times more than the pages I wrote for school. I simply flipped through the pages of worries, concerns, exciting moments, and heavy drama in the past years and drew inspiration from that. Then I sat down and wrote and wrote and wrote. Through much editing, out popped some pretty decent essays. My major two were about playing classical competitive piano (for fifteen years) and the struggle of having pride in being Chinese-American.

Originally, my intention was to write about my relationship with my mother, which would cover many of the Chinese pride topics. Yet in writing about it I realized that I was still living through this experience. One day I'd sit down to the computer and feel so frustrated and angry; the next day I'd feel like I understood my mom's values and where she was coming from. It was all too present in my life. So in the end, I decided to write about something from the past because I think one of the most important things is to be able to reflect on the topic you're writing about. And it did show in my final essay because I'd dealt with the issues of accepting my Chinese heritage and could clearly write about them and how they've influenced my life.

DON'T WHINE

Many of us choose to write our essays about a challenge or a traumatic experience we've overcome in our lives. Perhaps someone close to you died, or you were injured, or you moved around constantly as a kid, or you were bullied in junior high. When you're writing about a difficult experience, try not to dwell on the negative and sad emotions connected with it. Instead, focus on how this experience made you grow and develop as a unique person, what you learned from it and how what you learned changed your life.

Your goal is not to depress the admissions committee with a sob story, however touching it is. Your objective is to show how you're able to deal with challenges and what kind of person you've become as the result of a particular experience.

RE-WRITE YOUR INTRODUCTION

Your essay isn't the only one that the admissions committee is reading. There are hundreds or thousands more, and many that are written on similar topics. You can imagine that after a while they can all start to blend together. Your job is to break through the monotony and make your essay stand out. You need to grab the reader's attention with the first few sentences and then keep it throughout your essay.

That's why your introduction is so important and that's why our advice is to work on it extra hard. After you've written your essay, go back and re-read your introduction and ask yourself these questions:

- Does it grab the reader's attention with a strong opening sentence?

- Does it tell the reader what you're writing about and why this experience reveals something about you?

- Do you get to your main idea right away or are there sentences that drag on and are unnecessary?

- Do your introductory sentences make this essay sound like something you'd like to read?

- Have you avoided starting with a cliché or using a quote that doesn't do much to enhance your essay?

Spend some extra time on your intro and don't shy away from re-writing it if it doesn't grab the reader's attention and doesn't start your essay on a strong and memorable note.

REVISE CONTENT AND WRITING

We suggest that you do two sets of revisions for each essay. First, read your essay solely for its content. Focus on your ideas and their meaning, make sure that you're describing the what, why, and how of each experience, see that your essay is revealing something unique about you to the reader.

After you get comfortable with the overall content of your essay, focus on your writing. Admissions committees want to see how you communicate in writing so this is equally important. A poorly written essay, no matter how interesting, is difficult to read and won't make a good impression.

As you revise your writing, here are a few things to remember:

- **Connect your paragraphs**. Remember those transitions from English class? Even in a short piece of writing like your essay it's important to connect each paragraph and idea to the next. Otherwise, the writing appears choppy and the flow is hard to follow.

- **Use clear, punchy sentences**. Long-winded sentences and paragraphs are difficult to follow and they distract the reader from the essence of what you're trying to say. Read your sentences and make sure that each makes a strong point and does it with as few words as possible.

- **Vary your sentence length and structure**. Mix long and short sentences. Make sure all of your sentences don't sound the same. Make your writing interesting.

- **Check your grammar**. You're applying to college— needless to say you should write using correct grammar. If you feel uncertain about something, get some help. Even the smallest mistake can cost you the reader's attention.

- **Don't sound too formal**. Sometimes we adopt a more formal tone when we write as opposed to when we speak. While your essay shouldn't be written like a casual piece of conversation, it shouldn't sound like a stiff, academic article either. Read it out loud to yourself and see if it sounds like a smart person talking.

GET FEEDBACK AND ADVICE

"Have as many people as possible read your essay. It will give you many perspectives on how an admissions officer might view it."

**Freshman,
Emory University**

Essays are extremely important and you should get some feedback on yours from your parents, teachers, and counselors. Ask them to read your essays and give you their impressions and suggestions. Here are a few questions you might want to ask your essay readers to get as much useful feedback as possible:

- Was this essay interesting to read?

- What do you think I am trying to say?

- Was any part of it stronger than others? Weaker than others?

- What do you think I need to emphasize more? Less?

- Does my introduction do a good job of grabbing your attention?

- Does the writing style work? Is it too formal? Too casual?

Listening to criticism isn't always fun, but it can really help. Keep an open mind when getting feedback on your essays and while your own judgment is important, sometimes an independent reader can catch things that don't jump out at you.

> *"One of the hardest things, I think, is writing an essay about yourself and saying this is why I'm great. I felt like I had no accomplishments. My parents sat down with me and helped me write out the accomplishments that I'd made in my life. They thought of things I hadn't even thought of. Your parents are proud of you and even if the things you write seem cheesy to you, it's only because they're your own thing."*
>
> **Junior,**
> **Vassar College**

AVOID COMMON TRAPS

Here are a few common mistakes that many of us have made and you can hopefully avoid:

- **Don't wait until the last moment.** Writing essays takes time—to think, to organize your thoughts, to revise and re-write—and you won't have time for all these steps unless you leave yourself enough time. Plus, you'll feel rushed and anxious and your creative juices don't flow as well when you're under pressure.

- **Stay away from clichés.** It might seem convenient to call upon a cliché or two to help you express your feelings, but they sound fake and boring.

- **Don't overuse big words.** This is not an exercise to show how well you use a thesaurus. Write intelligently and naturally and sound like a human being. It's really difficult to express yourself honestly if you're trying to use big words that you don't normally use.

- **Say what you want, not what you think they want to hear.** The only thing admissions committees want to hear is you—writing in your own voice and expressing your own ideas. Be honest and be yourself.

> *"The people who read these things are quite perceptive and can smell the BS from a mile away."*
>
> **Recent Grad,**
> **Princeton University**

- **Take a breath between drafts.** You need to give your brain some time to chill out before you go back to your essays to revise them. Leave a few days, or even weeks, between drafts and you'll come back with a fresh and more critical eye.

WRITE SOMETHING MEANINGFUL

by
Mike Yank
Recent Grad, Harvard University

When I sat down to brainstorm ideas for my college application essays, I started second guessing myself endlessly. I kept trying to figure out what I needed to write so that they would accept me. In particular, the openness of personal statement questions frustrated me, since I didn't know if I should write about an impressive accomplishment or not. It seemed like an impossible task, and everything I wrote at first sounded clichéd, so I had to start over.

Ultimately, I ended up writing about a very mundane experience that meant a lot to me: the time my parents bought me an accordion. I realized that my accomplishments and various qualifications would come out through other aspects of my application, so I used the essay as a chance to show off a distinctive part of my personality. Everyone else applying to these schools would also have a remarkable achievement to write about, I reasoned, so why try to make myself look distinctive by talking about the day I won a special prize?

I like to think that my essay made me stand out from the other applicants, not because it let the admissions officers know that I have a certain talent, but because I took the opportunity to share a unique detail of my life that meant a lot to me.

PROOFREAD LIKE A MANIAC

You've put a great deal of effort into your essays—don't let a spelling mistake distract the reader and take away from your great work. Take time to proofread your writing and after you think it's perfect, proofread it again. This is definitely an area where you can't do too much.

Never rely on your computer's spell-check and grammar check. They miss many mistakes, such as when you need to use their vs. there. Go over every sentence slowly and carefully, checking every word and every grammar structure. Check commas, periods, capitalization, word repetition, verbs and tenses, nouns, and number agreements. You've done this dozens of times for your high school papers and you have the skills to get it right. The key is to spend enough time and have the patience to go through every word and every sentence.

If possible, ask your parents and your English teacher to proofread your essay. There's nothing like another pair of eyes to check your work.

☞ A WORD ON PROFESSIONAL EDITING SERVICES

There are many companies and online services that promise to edit your college essays to perfection. Should you use them? As with everything else we've written about here, it's your personal choice. If you're having a hard time, don't have much support from your family, teachers, and guidance counselors, you might find value in having someone else read and make suggestions for your essay. But what you always want to avoid is having someone else re-write or, worse, write your essay for you. Even if you pull it off and get in with an essay written by someone else, just imagine how awful it will feel to know that it wasn't your own work.

If you do decide to use an editing service, do some legwork to make sure that it's a legitimate operation staffed by professional editors who know something about writing and college essays. One of the most popular services is an online company called **www.EssayEdge.com**. Its editors are all Harvard students and graduates and the company offers a few levels of service from reading your essays and making some general comments to proofreading your work. Students who've used it seem to like the value they got for their money, but you should do your own research.

There are also companies that sell college essays. Here we're pretty passionate about our advice—stay away. You're smart enough to write your own essays. And admissions officers are astute and have good memories—if they think your essay is not your own work, you can count on getting a rejection.

ESSAY EXAMPLES

There are a few great books out there that include dozens of actual college essays that were part of successful applications to everywhere from Ivy League schools to state universities. (50 Essays That Worked, published by Fawcett Books, is probably one of the most popular.) If you're stuck or want to get familiar with what type of essays students write you might want to pick up a book like that. Do keep in mind that the essays presented there are only a few examples and you don't have to—and shouldn't—write on any similar topics or in a similar style.

For the same purpose of giving you a general idea of what a college essay might look like, we've included a few on the following pages. Each one was part of a successful college application and each one is unique in its own way. Hopefully reading through a few examples will help you see some of the things we've mentioned in this chapter actually presented in an essay.

Essay #1
Successful application essay to Pomona College

It was a brisk spring morning in mid-April. It began like any other morning. I got ready for school and picked up my book bag, but I already knew that today was different. Today was "Moving Up Day," the day when every eighth grader would first step into the upper school. We were afraid of what was to come.

Science was my first class. A pack of eighth graders timidly stepped into the huge room. Each of us claimed a stool around the long table. The scale of the room, however, hardly compared to the scale of the man who would follow us into it. Mr. Gruber may be thin, but he is enormously tall. At 6'3", he dwarfed even the most mature middle-schooler.

Mr. Gruber told us how we would get to explore many realms of science in "Foundations" class next year. He talked about physics and chemistry, biology and geology, and the connections between each of these disciplines. To end his class, he asked us to name any two objects for him to relate. He showed us how the room's ceiling proves the existence of life on earth, and how the ocean has everything to do with a simple desk lamp. I walked away from that room with the realization that everything is intimately connected.

Mr. Gruber's Moving Up Day speech would express itself many times throughout my high school years. Most directly, it affected the way I thought about my education. I was emboldened to cross disciplinary boundaries, bringing Science into English class and Math into History. The story of Pyramus and Thisbe, for example, was not only relevant in Latin. Ovid actually helped me to understand Shakespeare in literature and Rome in history. Similarly, learning about the distinction between Romanticism and the Enlightenment in history gave me a deeper understanding of Mary Shelley's *Frankenstein* in literature.

This interdisciplinary approach also influenced my choice of employment. During the summer of 2000, still intrigued by the idea of connecting disciplines, I had the opportunity to cross technology with history and political science. I sought out Professor Ian Lustick, Chair of the Political Science Department at the University of Pennsylvania. Professor Lustick developed a dynamic systems model to predict the ways in which dominant and minority ideas interact and spread throughout cultures. In areas of conflict like Israel and Ireland, majority and minority views are always in flux. Whose ideas will win out? At what point will these ideas be stable enough to control future political influence? With Professor Lustick and his graduate students, I tested computer simulation models against current political theories—theories that may someday be used to determine the course of politics. None of this would have been possible if Mr. Gruber had not awakened me to the process of seeing connectedness and interrelationships.

Since that time, my classmates and I have come to believe that Mr. Gruber is omniscient. For any question, he seems to come up with a logical and well-reasoned answer that melds together information from multiple sources. As I move forward in life, I am convinced that Mr. Gruber's lesson, on that fateful day, may be the foundation on which my intellectual future rests. Though I am sure to forget the names of every anatomical muscle of the cat and rabbit, Mr. Gruber's lesson that "the more you learn, the more you realize how little you know" will always remain with me. Only by learning to think, to analyze, to question and to form insights can we truly begin to understand the connections between things. These are the skills and processes upon which a lifetime of learning is based.

Essay strengths:

- *Shows intellectual drive and passion for learning.*
- *Eloquently written and organized.*
- *Writer seems genuinely touched and influenced by this experience.*

Could improve:

- *The essay takes a while to get to its core point and could be made punchier with a more direct introduction.*

Essay #2
Successful application essay to Middlebury College

In third grade, I was the only American in my school. Housed within ten foot concrete walls, a steel door, and covered with graffiti, the Sir James Henderson British School of Milan, Italy, possessed anything but a welcoming appearance. Inside, the atmosphere was no different. When the Gulf War came about, I spent weeks at home or in the mountains, unable to attend school because of recurring bomb threats. Time spent at school meant bodyguards with machine guns in the playground. After the American Bookstore half a block away from my apartment was bombed, I was ordered not to speak in public. Bus and subway rides, walks to and from school, and weekend museum trips were spent in silence. Essentially I had to discover a way to blend into several different environments and cultures, while at the same time maintaining my own sense of identity. In retrospect, I realize that perhaps I did not fully understand the extent of the opportunities I was faced with during these three years, namely the opportunity for world travel. It has taken time to understand the impact of this time with respect to the person I am now.

I was born in Mexico City, then moved to Singapore, then to America, then to Italy and finally back to where I am currently living in Pennsylvania. My father's childhood followed much of the same story, jumping from one country to another. For these reasons, though the feeling is much stronger now, I have always felt uprooted and perhaps in some ways dispossessed. Approached with the seemingly simple question: "Where are you from?" I often balk. Instead of an answer, I deliver a barrage of questions, for I have no true answer. These travels have left me lost in some aspects, but without them I would be just as lost. I never expected to feel culture shock in America, yet when I came back I found I had missed out on simple things that set me apart from other children. Having spent years on a concrete playground in Italy, I had no concept of dodge ball or mat ball. Though small, these little differences created the kind of alienation I felt initially upon my arrival in Milan. In the classroom at Sir James Henderson I was often put in the position as *the* American opinion, *the* American voice, many times speaking from a defensive standpoint.

It was in these disputes with my elders and peers that I gained the ability to speak strongly and with conviction. If I seemed unsure in my arguments, there was no chance of convincing others.

My cultural dilemma was certainly shared, though in many beneficial ways. Gathering friends from Israel, France, Greece, and Britain, to name a few, we all gave to each other and took as well, learning in ways in which we were not even aware. Though a shock, being thrown into cultures different from mine at such a young age has created the core of my person. These travels and the experiences that I have gained from them have become an intrinsic part of me. Though in many ways one could argue that patriotism has declined in the youth of today, there is an undeniable comfort in the ability to attach oneself to a certain culture or group. This is something for which I have searched, yet have been unable to find. Through discussion I discovered I shared these same sentiments with my sister, who, faced with the issue of college, solved this problem by studying in Scotland.

Initially I thought that that path would be the right one for me as well. While visiting colleges in the UK, I knew that I had been wrong in my assumptions. I was not American and yet I was not European either. I needed to find a middle ground. Through the cultures I had experienced, I had found common themes throughout. I could not attach myself to one specific culture because each had an attribute I was seeking, but also lacked other important components. I sought a place that managed to combine these themes in a way that was welcoming and complete. At the universities I explored in England, I found a clear lean towards one culture, one way of thinking and doing. Immersing myself in this university would have meant devoting myself to one culture and limiting my exposure to others. Many of the colleges I visited in the United States projected much the same mindset. It was at Middlebury that I found that which I had been seeking. The emphasis on foreign languages, the strength of the study abroad programs, and the presence of foreign language houses clearly indicated that Middlebury placed the same value in multiculturalism as I myself did. For these specific reasons I felt as if attending Middlebury would not mean sacrificing my values and need for international exposure. Serving as a representative for America for three years gave me strength, confidence, and courage.

I feel more balanced and more knowledgeable than I would have otherwise. New and different perspectives, though sometimes gained through difficult lessons and taking risks, have made me capable of interaction with a wide variety of personalities and cultures. I have been forced to truly question myself, my motives, my priorities, and my position. These conflicting viewpoints and cultures have guided me into examining my beliefs and given me the conviction to assert and firmly root myself, if not in a specific culture, then in a specific philosophy of living.

Essay strengths:

- *Tells the admissions committee about the very unique life perspectives this applicant would bring.*
- *Shows how the experiences in the applicant's life lead her to choose Middlebury as her selected college.*
- *Reads like an honest account of the writer's feelings and thoughts.*

Could improve:

- *This essay could be shortened by working through each sentence and eliminating any words that don't contribute directly to the point being made.*

Essay #3
Successful application essay to the University of Portland

Upon my four years as a student of Sandy High School I have had numerous people enter my life and just as many exit. But through this growing process there is one individual, a teacher, I hold in high regard that has helped me expand my understanding of writing, revealing the art that it is.

I entered his Advanced Composition class as a naïve sophomore, believing I had everything under control. Writing was something that had always come naturally to me, allowing me to move swiftly through past English courses without hindrance. My misguided assumption was abruptly transposed into a blood-chilling fear for my very life. He walked into the classroom and announced in a calm patient voice, that seemed to be hiding something behind it, "My name is Roger Shepard, you will address me as Mr. Shepard, you may not call me Roger until you graduate and if you do this is what will happen to you." As he said this he raised a large cane into the air above his head and slammed it on the desk nearest him. He continued, "I expect to receive nothing less than perfection relating to your papers and you have a paper due tomorrow morning discussing what writing is to you. Remember, perfection..." Thus ended my first day of Advanced Composition, I wanted to die.

My papers were far from perfect and Mr. Shepard became my worst critic. He urged me to reach higher, push myself harder, and put more effort into my work. Every paper I presented to him, he could rip it apart. Even the papers I thought were immaculate could not survive the expectations of that man. In my mind he slowly transformed into an Advanced Composition god, one that would never be appeased with the tainted offerings of his feeble-witted worshippers.

But as time went by I began to realize that every piece of criticism he presented me with was with my best interests at hand, always; everything he told me was for the betterment of me and my work, helping to guide me towards higher learning. As I started to apply his critiques my papers improved gradually, they were in constant growth throughout the remainder of the year.

That class was the most difficult of my high school career and it was because of him, the crazed god of Composition. He pushed my writing abilities far beyond anything I had ever hoped to achieve alone. He understood that my knack for writing could be cultivated into something much bigger and more useful to me later in life. But most importantly, he was willing to put time and effort into the gift he saw in me. Mr. Shepard taught me never to be satisfied with the mediocre and to always strive to do my best at everything.

Essay strengths:

- *The introduction is direct and tells the admissions committee what this essay is about.*
- *Honestly-written and sounds like the applicant talking rather than overusing big words that don't seem natural.*
- *Shows the applicant's passion for hard work.*

Could improve:

- *The writing in the essay is sometimes choppy and could benefit from a few revisions focused specifically on sentence structure and word choice.*

❶ ❷

get
great recs

Most colleges require two or three recommendations to be included with your application. Like a good essay, a good recommendation is an extremely influential part of your admissions package. It can share valuable insight into your strengths and unique qualities and it makes you come alive as a person beyond your grades and test scores.

Despite what you may think, you can have an impact on the quality of your recommendations. By choosing your references carefully and making sure that you give them enough time, you can maximize your chances of getting stellar recommendations.

CHOOSE THE RIGHT PEOPLE
▼
BE PROFESSIONAL
▼
SAY THANK YOU
▼
DON'T GO OVERBOARD

CHOOSE THE RIGHT PEOPLE

> *"The key to getting good recs is not to pick the teacher of the class where you did the best, or the English teacher who you know can crank out wonderful prose, though these things might be helpful. Try to pick someone who truly knows you as a person, rather than just as a student. The recommendations you get from these teachers are always the best."*
>
> **Sophomore,**
> **Brown University**

The person writing your letter of recommendation should know you well and should think positively of your academic performance and of you as a person. Teachers whose classes you've taken and who've witnessed your development are great resources, as well as guidance counselors who've seen you tackle challenges and grow as you overcame them.

> *"I had a recommender who had me in class for a couple of years. He knew me as a person as well as a student and could comment on my character as well as my academic abilities."*
>
> **Recent Grad,**
> **Smith College**

When you begin to think about who will write your letters, a few names will probably spring to mind. Don't rush, though, and give each one some thought.

- Does this person know you well enough to comment on your abilities as a student and your character as a person? For example, even though your former biology teacher may be a twenty-four year old assistant coach of your soccer team who gave you straight A's, he might not be as qualified and experienced in writing recommendations as your near-retirement, hard-nosed English teacher whose respect you earned by working hard to get B's.

- Have you maintained a strong relationship with this person or is this a teacher from your freshman-year English class with whom you haven't spoken in a few years?

- Does this person generally write in an eloquent and easy-to-read style? You want to avoid people who're overly verbose as well as those that are too curt. (This is tough to judge, but think about comments you might've received on your papers or exams.)

> *"There are two parts to this: Your recommenders must be able to write well and they must be able to write good things about you."*
>
> **Recent Grad,**
> **Princeton University**

As you think about your choices, make sure that they're diverse enough. It's not a great idea to get two recommendations from two of your English teachers, for example.

Some colleges will require one of your recommendations to come from your guidance counselor. Keep this in mind as you go through your junior and senior years and try to get to know your counselor as well as possible. Make appointments to talk about your college goals, get advice about your college choices, and discuss essay topics and financial aid issues. The better your counselor knows you the better his or her letter of recommendation will be.

As for people who you shouldn't ask for a recommendation, it's your family and relatives. They love you and think the world of you, but they're not appropriate as college references. Instead, use their feedback and support in other areas, such as working with you on your essays.

BE PROFESSIONAL

No matter how highly your references think of you, handing them recommendation forms the day before they're due is a quick and sure-fire way to make them sour. To play it safe, you should give your references at least one month to write a recommendation and send it in. Asking early shows that you're organized and are respectful of their time. In addition, just as you don't want to rush your own essays, you don't want your teachers to rush their recommendations. Giving your teachers extra time will allow them to develop their ideas and write the most effective letters.

When asking someone for a letter of recommendation be as professional as possible:

- Schedule an appointment to make your request and tell your references how highly you value their opinion and how much you appreciate their effort. Remember, they're probably writing more than just your recommendation and each one takes significant time from their already busy schedule.

- Be very clear about the deadline for sending in the recommendation and always, always leave ample time for your teacher to write it.

- Give your recommenders every piece of required information so that they don't have to waste time hunting for it. This includes: at least two copies of the forms the recommender needs to fill out (one for a rough draft), stamped and addressed envelope to send the recommendation, your name, address, and social security number (you will usually fill these in on the recommendation form itself).

- Think about giving copies of your essays to the teachers and counselors writing your letters. They might find it helpful to have some additional information about you, some of which they might not have known before.

You have the option of maintaining the right to see your completed recommendation forms, but without a doubt you should waive your right to do this. This demonstrates to your references that you trust them to write honestly and sincerely about you. Also, it shows admissions officers that your references' opinions are honest and uninfluenced, which makes them much more credible.

Follow up with your recommenders a few weeks before the deadline for sending in the letters to make sure that they're on track. A good way to do this without being pushy is to ask them if there is any other information that you could provide for them. As long as you're polite, most won't mind a little prodding.

"*The worst way to ask for a recommendation is to leave it to the last minute, ask a teacher via email rather than in person, assume that the teacher will automatically say yes, or forget to include the right forms and stamped, addressed envelopes. It's also rather poor form not to say thank you and not to let the teacher know where you're headed next year.*"

**Co-Principal,
Friends Central School**

WE TALK WITH...

Ben Cohen-Leadholm
Recent Grad, Wesleyan University

What was your plan for asking teachers and advisors for recommendations? Did it work?

When I decided to apply to Yale Early Action I knew I needed to bring out the big guns. So I selected teachers who would literally fall all over themselves about me in their recommendations, like my Spanish teacher whom I'd know since I was thirteen and who would still reference presentations I'd given in the 8th grade.

Then I got rejected from Yale. So I Xeroxed copies of my rejection letter for each person who had "helped" me, and I told them it was their fault. Okay, I didn't. I took a deep breath and then applied to eight more schools.

How many teachers did you ask?

I probably asked five teachers, which is plenty. Since I applied to nine schools in total, I actually felt bad asking that each person write so many recommendations.

Any advice on what to do to get great recs?

Make it a one-stop deal for your teachers and counselors. If your favorite Calculus teacher will be writing recommendations for all seven of your schools, give him a folder with everything clearly labeled and paper-clipped. Include addressed, postage-paid envelopes. These people are doing you an enormous favor—make it as simple and painless a process as you can for them.

SAY THANK YOU

"Ask really nicely when seeking faculty recommendations and make the entire process as easy as possible for your teachers. Hand them pre-addressed, stamped envelopes, and make sure they know you appreciate their efforts. I included a bag of chocolate-covered espresso beans with my forms to each teacher, just to say thank you. Don't go overboard though—there's a fine line between thanks and bribery."

**Senior,
Columbia University**

When someone agrees to write you a letter of recommendation you should thank them and express how much you appreciate their help. When they send out your letters, you should write a more formal thank-you note. This is a great gesture that teachers and counselors definitely appreciate and it shows that you really value their efforts.

"Good relationships are always important in life, so remember to express your gratitude to your recommenders when it's all over. They are, after all, doing you a significant favor."

**Recent Grad,
Princeton University**

DON'T GO OVERBOARD

Should you send in more letters of recommendation than a college requires? If only two letters are required, but there are three people that you feel all have different and valuable perspectives about you as a student and as a person, it will not hurt your chances to get an extra letter of recommendation. If all three are great, or if one is not as strong as you thought it would be, this can even help you.

What you should avoid is going overboard and sending in five letters when only two are required. This suggests that you aren't confident in your recommendations and that's the reverse of what you want to demonstrate to the admissions committee.

Colleges differ with their views on extra recommendations, so it might not be a bad idea to call up and ask about any specific policies.

13

impress
your interviewers

For most schools, the interview is an optional part of the application process. But it's such a great opportunity to both enhance your application and find out more about the school that we definitely suggest you interview with as many colleges as possible. Sure, it might be somewhat intimidating and not all interviewers are as friendly as you'd like, but it's worth the extra effort.

And don't feel alone if you're stressed out at the prospect of meeting one-on-one with a person who might impact your acceptance chances—we've all been there. Try to focus on the interview as being a two-sided dialogue and keep in mind that even if it goes poorly, it won't single-handedly affect the outcome of your application.

AS NIKE SAYS…JUST DO IT
▼
DO SOME HOMEWORK
▼
NAIL THE LOGISTICS
▼
DON'T OVERDRESS
▼
BE YOURSELF
▼
MAINTAIN A DIALOGUE
▼
FOLLOW UP

AS NIKE SAYS...JUST DO IT

If you're uncertain about whether to do an interview with a member of the admissions committee, a student, or an alumni interviewer, our advice is: Do it. The risk you face from an interview gone bad is low because it's just one component of your college application and can't single-handedly determine the outcome. But the potential benefits are significant:

- You get to put a face and a personality to a bunch of papers with your grades, scores, and essays. This is the one shot that you have to be a person rather than a collection of application materials.

- If there's anything about your application to which you need to give context—say, low grades during your sophomore year when your close friend was sick—this is your opportunity to do it.

- Doing an interview shows that you're really interested in the college and are willing to put in the extra effort to enhance your application.

- An interview is a dialogue and you get to ask questions—this is a great time to get a feel for what the staff or alumni are like and to find out any specific information that might impact your decision.

So go ahead and schedule an interview. You might have to conduct an alumni interview if the school is too far away to travel or if its schedule is overbooked. While alumni interviews hold somewhat less weight than admissions officers' interviews, they have many of the same benefits.

WE TALK WITH...

Rachel Skerritt
Recent Grad, University of Pennsylvania

Were you nervous about your college interviews?

I think everyone is nervous when facing a grown-up who could decide a big part of your future. I'm not a shy person, so I was probably less nervous than others, but at the same time I REALLY wanted to go to UPenn, so this interview was the most important one I'd ever had.

Did it go well?

My interview was one of the most positive high school experiences I've ever had. After the first twenty minutes, I honestly forgot everything that was on the line. It felt like it was a real conversation and not a pressure-filled Q & A. I met my interviewer at a coffee shop and we stayed there for two hours. We didn't end up talking about any of the things I thought we would—why I want to go to Penn, what my best qualities are, etc. Instead, we talked all about *The Who's Tommy*, the musical I'd just seen the day before.

What interview advice can you share?

Smile and have a good time. Enthusiasm is contagious, but you can't be fake. Allow your personality to shine through. Show your interviewer the utmost respect without being so formal that the whole situation feels uncomfortable.

Feel free to tell a story about a social situation that you were in, but don't include things that teenagers shouldn't be doing. Think of a couple of anecdotes that you'd like to discuss at the interview—things that make you distinct and interesting. That way, no matter what comes up, you can find ways to slip in those fun and memorable tidbits about yourself.

DO SOME HOMEWORK

The best way to prepare for an interview is to anticipate the questions you might be asked and to think about your responses ahead of time. Here are some common ones:

- Why do you want to go to this school?
- What other schools are you considering?
- What are you thinking of studying?
- What do you think are your strengths and weaknesses?
- So I see on your application that you are active in (insert an activity)—tell me more about it.
- What were some of your favorite classes this year?
- I read your essay about (insert your topic)—tell me more about that.

Your interviewer will most often have a copy of your application and your essays, so you can expect a lot of questions to be based on the information you included. Definitely think about your essay topics and your extracurriculars and how you might talk about them during the interview.

If you can, try to get some basic information about your interviewer. For example, how long the person has worked at the school, does he or she teach any classes or supervise any extracurricular clubs or organizations. For alumni, know when they graduated and perhaps what they studied in college. The more you know about your interviewer the more comfortable you'll be. Plus, you can ask much better questions in the area where you know your interviewer is knowledgeable (e.g., if your alumni interviewer majored in chemistry and that's an area you're interested in, you have a great area for discussion).

NAIL THE LOGISTICS

There are enough horror stories about arriving late to interviews, getting lost, missing the appointment, and so on that you don't need to add yours to the pile. Make sure to do the following:

- Know where you're going.

- Always allow extra time for travel delays, like traffic.

- Plan to get to your destination at least twenty minutes early so you can catch your breath, relax, and focus instead of figuring out where to park your car.

- Bring the phone number of the place where you're meeting your interviewer and always call ahead to confirm. (You should also call ahead if you're running late.)

- Bring a copy of your resume, application, and essays with you. If the interviewer doesn't have them but wants to take a look, you'll be prepared.

DON'T OVERDRESS

"You want to be dressier than casual, but you don't have to be uncomfortable."

**Recent Grad,
Smith College**

Your goal for the interview is to make a good impression within a short amount of time and that starts with your appearance. While there's no need to buy a new suit for a college interview, you should look nice and professional.

For guys, this means slacks or khakis with a nice collared shirt, and perhaps a tie. For gals, a nice blouse with a skirt or nice pants works well. Definitely skip jeans, shorts, t-shirts, long sleeve t-shirts, or any overly crazy and funky clothing. Showing your personality is important, but you shouldn't do it through your clothes.

Remember that your interview can take place in any number of settings—from the living room of a local alumnus to an office building to a university's admissions office. Take a cue from the venue on how to dress, but remember that in an interview situation you're better off being slightly overdressed than underdressed.

Make sure that you feel comfortable in your interview outfit. If you normally don't wear suits it might feel strange to be wearing one and you may get distracted.

Megan's corner
▼

I woke up later than I wanted to the morning of one of my interviews and ended up scrambling around the hotel room, climbing under the bed, and looking for my other sock. For the sake of punctuality over fashion, I ended up going to my interview with an ankle-cut white athletic sock on one foot and an orange and red striped knee-high sock on the other. I got into the school, but I don't know how impressed the interviewer was with my fashion sense. Lay your clothes out the night before. This might sound like something your mother made you do in kindergarten, but anything you can do to make your morning less stressful is definitely a good thing.
▲

BE YOURSELF

"My interviewers ranged from 'wow this guy is awesome!' to 'T-minus fifteen minutes until this painful experience is over.' Try to be relaxed and honest. It's not as if these people are trying to humiliate you. They simply want to bring out your character."

**Recent Grad,
Princeton University**

The interview is your shot to show what you're like in person—don't waste it by trying to be some way that you think you're supposed to be. You're you and you're who the interviewer is interested in meeting. Be honest, be open, be yourself, and remember that there's no right way to do this.

This "be yourself" advice sounds like a big cliché, but it's really important. When you try to make yourself sound like someone else, you get anxious and stressed and risk having an interview that's stiff and not so great. If you relax and have confidence in your ability to be an impressive candidate, things will go much more smoothly.

Here's an example:

Say you're involved in Amnesty International at your high school. Your friend made you go to the first few meetings but you stuck with it because you learned about the organization and wanted to support its goals.

When the interviewer asks you why you got involved with Amnesty International, you might think that the best response is something like: "I've always cared about human rights and wanted to do my part to promote them through Amnesty International." If that were true, great, but in this scenario, it's much better to be honest and to say that you initially got involved because of your friend but became interested in Amnesty's mission and wanted to continue working with it. This response sounds genuine, and when you're being genuine you'll come off in a much more persuasive way.

> "Be yourself is one of the biggest clichés in existence so I'm going to amend it to 'Be a slightly better version of yourself.' Wear something neat and comfortable. Even if you aren't generally talkative, try to be open and honest with your interviewer. Reveal things about yourself—what you like and enjoy, and what's important to you. Be animated and be funny, if you want."
>
> **Freshman,**
> **Brown University**

MAINTAIN A DIALOGUE

> "I enjoyed most of my interviews. When I didn't get nervous about an interview and just thought of it as going in to meet a new person—not so much as going in to get attacked by a person who was going to determine my future—things went really well. We'd talk naturally and often I wished the conversation would go on past our time constraint. So try to make the interview like a dialogue. Think of yourself as an equal with your interviewer and you'll remain relaxed and come off more confident."
>
> **Freshman,**
> **Harvard University**

An interview is not an interrogation, it's a dialogue. You're here to talk with your interviewer and talking means sometimes taking the lead and asking questions. Asking questions is important to keep the balance of the interview even, and to show that you've given this school and interview some thought and have a genuine interest in finding out more.

You should definitely prepare a few questions in advance to have in your back pocket if you get nervous or stuck. Make sure to ask things that aren't obvious or those that you could've found out by simply going to the school's website. For example, "How many students go to this school?" is not as impressive as asking something more specific like: "I've read that 60% of all students go abroad and I was wondering what kind of programs are available and supported by the college?"

It's also a good idea to ask your interviewer some questions about his or her personal experience with the school, especially if you're interviewing with an alumnus or a student. Here are some ideas:

- What do you think are some of the best things about this school?

- I know that you majored in (x)—what did you think about that program? Is it a strong department?

- I'm not sure if a large or a small school is the right choice for me—how was your experience and do you have any suggestions?

- I'm thinking of majoring in (x)—do you know any professors from that department and what do you think about them?

You'll probably think of some questions as you're talking and it's completely fine to follow the flow of conversation—don't feel like there are things that you're supposed to ask.

When you do ask a question, make sure that you carefully listen to the response and look interested in what the person is saying. If it looks like you're asking a question for the sake of asking it you'll lose more than you gain.

FOLLOW UP

Always follow up after your interview. It's appropriate to send a thank-you note by mail, saying that you appreciate the person taking the time to meet with you and you enjoyed your conversation.

If there was something specific that you discussed during the interview, or if your interviewer suggested that you investigate a certain aspect of the school in detail, you might want to mention it and add a personal touch to your thank-you letter.

"We call them interviews, but they are really just opportunities for us to get to know the students and for the students to get to know us. I'm always impressed when students come to interviews dressed nicely and are prepared to answer questions about their high school experience—both academics and extracurriculars."

Admissions Counselor,
Butler University

MY COLLEGE INTERVIEW

by
Greg Guenthner
Senior, George Mason University

I didn't know what to expect when I applied to college. All I knew was that I wanted to go somewhere different, a place where my friends weren't applying. I applied to all public schools, so nearly all of them didn't require an interview. When I received a letter in the mail from George Mason reminding me to schedule an interview date, I'd almost decided not to go to the trouble of making the three-hour drive just to be grilled about my below-average grades in trigonometry. But my parents convinced me to give it a chance, so my father and I drove to the university the following weekend.

So there I was, nervous and dressed in a tie and sports jacket, waiting for my name to be called for the interview. I looked around the waiting room filled with applicants in jeans or polo shirts and I realized I was a little overdressed, which didn't exactly help my nerves. While a thousand thoughts ran through my head, my name was called and I made my way to the interview room. I was greeted by a friendly alumnus who informed me that she would be conducting my interview. I breathed a sigh of relief and took my seat.

To my surprise, the interview went great. The alum was nice and asked me all about my hiking trip to New Mexico about which I wrote my essay. She told me about her experience at the university and things to think about when finally deciding where to spend the next four years of my life. After we talked for almost an hour, she gave me a list of people to contact about answers to my questions regarding the communication department. She also thanked me for dressing nicely and wished me good luck on my college search.

I was just happy she didn't bring up trigonometry.

14

get the most money for college

The one thing that we can tell you for certain about financial aid is that you have to work hard to get it. It would be nice if it all worked out on its own and someone came to your door with a full four-year scholarship, but that doesn't happen. You have to fill out forms, keep track of deadlines, check into dozens of resources, and do this not just before you go to college, but also while you're there. It's work and it's tiring, but persistence does pay off.

The advice in this chapter is excerpted from a Students Helping Students™ book called **GETTING THROUGH COLLEGE WITHOUT GOING BROKE**. You should definitely check it out for much more detailed advice on financial aid, scholarships, budgeting for college, working and studying, learning to manage money at school, dealing with credit cards and debt, and much more.

START EARLY
▼
TALK TO YOUR GUIDANCE COUNSELOR
▼
NAIL THE FAFSA
▼
ACE YOUR SCHOLARSHIP APPLICATONS
▼
NAVIGATE THE LOAN MAZE
▼
DON'T MISS DEADLINES
▼
LOOK UNDER EVERY ROCK
▼
DON'T RELY ON YOUR PARENTS

START EARLY

The sooner you start looking for money for college and filling out applications and forms, the better off you'll be. No question. If you and your parents file taxes early in the year, instead of waiting until April, you'll have the most up-to-date information about the state of your family's finances for the FAFSA and PROFILE forms. Writing scholarship essays early will let you be more relaxed, and will give you time to have your mom, your little brother, your English teacher, and anyone else who's willing read them over and make them better. Some scholarships also have early deadlines, and you don't want to miss out on extra cash just because you didn't find out about it in time.

You should start learning about all of the available financial aid options during your junior year, and be ready to write your scholarship essays and submit applications by the first semester of your senior year. It's not a bad idea to write a few scholarship essays during the summer after your junior year, and if you're working on your college essays at the same time, you can probably re-use some of the material. You'll fill out your FAFSA and PROFILE forms at the beginning of your second semester senior year, and you'll get your financial aid offers around the same time as your college acceptance letters in the spring.

TALK TO YOUR GUIDANCE COUNSELOR

It is your guidance counselor's job to help you plan for college and advise you on how to pay for it. Guidance counselors have lists of local and national scholarships, as well as resources for searching for scholarships. From the experience of working with many other students they also know which colleges are more likely to give you a decent financial aid package, and they can recommend to you where to look for other financing options.

Set up a meeting with your guidance counselor during your junior year to talk about your plan of attack to find money for college, and continue to meet with him or her throughout the process. The more you talk to your counselor, the more he or she will remember your name, and the more he or she will realize your determination to find a way to pay for college. Your counselor will remember this when he or she is meeting with local scholarship committees, and it can help you in the long run.

> *"I talked often with my guidance counselor about my family's fear of not being able to pay for college. It must have stuck in her mind because she kept telling me about all these scholarships, and even recommended me for some of them."*
>
> **Recent Grad,**
> **Wesleyan University**

NAIL THE FAFSA

Even if you don't think that you'll be eligible for financial aid, you should apply. It can't hurt to try, and you won't have a shot at any aid if you don't file the required applications. You don't have to be poor to receive financial aid, and many families lose out on thousands of dollars in loans and scholarships because they think they have too much money to qualify. Don't miss out on aid that can save you thousands.

"My parents did most of the filling in of financial aid forms, but I wish I had done more. Now that I'm paying hundreds of dollars a month to pay back the loans, I feel like the band that never read the fine print and was signed to a bad record deal."

Recent Grad,
University of Wisconsin – Madison

The first and most important thing you need to do is fill out the **Free Application for Federal Student Aid**—or, as it's widely known, the FAFSA.

- This is the bedrock of all financial aid forms—without it you can't get any aid at all—so it's extremely important that you file it on-time and accurately. There is no filing fee, and you can file this form online if you wish. We suggest that you take the opportunity to file the FAFSA electronically by going to **www.fafsa.ed.gov**. You'll get your Student Aid Report sooner and since the online form has internal checks built in, you'll avoid careless errors. If you do want to fill out the paper version, you can usually get it from your school or by calling 1-800-4-FED-AID.

- You need to re-file the FAFSA every year that you are in school in order to be considered for federal student aid, including grants, loans and work-study programs. Often schools use this form to determine non-federal aid as well. A change in your family's financial situation may increase or decrease the amount of aid you're receiving, and even if you didn't qualify one year you might be eligible for aid the following year.

- You should file the FAFSA early during the second semester of your senior year. You can't file it before January 1—you need to give the government the full picture of your family's financial situation for the most recent fiscal year—but you should file it soon after that. The Department of Education will process FAFSA forms all year while you're in college, but most school aid is distributed on a first-come-first-serve basis, so it's in your interest to apply early. In addition, each school has a different priority deadline, many as early as February or March, and you need to meet that deadline to get your full potential aid. It's not necessary to submit your and your parents' tax return to the IRS before submitting your FAFSA, but since you will need some important information from your and your parents' taxes while filling it out, you should try to complete them beforehand.

- The FAFSA asks for details of your finances from both you and your parents, but you don't have to turn in your actual tax forms to your school or with the FAFSA. To ensure honesty, however, colleges do random audits where they check your information, and you risk losing all your aid if the information you supply to FAFSA does not match your filed tax forms.

It takes about six weeks for your FAFSA to be processed, and you'll then be sent a **Student Aid Report (SAR)**. This report can look a bit confusing, but it's not so bad. The front page will have the date and something called the **Expected Family Contribution** (EFC), which will be followed by a number. That number is the amount of dollars that your family will be expected to contribute to your college education each year. The lower the amount, the more aid you'll likely receive. Here's an easy way to think about it:

Financial Need=Cost of Attendance–Expected Contribution

However, having a low expected contribution does not guarantee full aid. If your EFC is only $500, but you're applying to schools that cost $20,000, don't necessarily expect your financial aid package to fully cover the difference.

> *"My parents gasped when they looked at the expected contribution—it seemed ridiculously high. It was kind of panicky for a while, but we talked to the school where I really wanted to go, explained our circumstances, and they were able to give me some loans. Not ideal, but it was a solution."*

> **Recent Grad,**
> **Wesleyan University**

Make sure you read your SAR carefully and review it for any errors you may have made. If you note any errors, make corrections on Part 2 of the form and mail it back promptly—you'll receive a new SAR. The federal processor of the FAFSA will send a copy of your SAR to each of the schools that you listed on the FAFSA and they will use it to calculate your financial aid package.

Some schools require further paperwork than the FAFSA. They'll ask that you fill out their custom form or something called the PROFILE. The PROFILE is also administered by the College Board and is used by many private colleges to determine your eligibility for non-governmental loans such as those provided by the school itself. The PROFILE is more in-depth than the FAFSA and uses a different methodology to calculate your financial need. To file the PROFILE online, go to **www.CollegeBoard.org**. Make sure to check with each of the schools to which you're applying to see if you need to file a PROFILE, or if there are any other forms you should worry about.

Many high schools offer information sessions for seniors on applying for aid and filling out the proper forms. If yours does, take advantage of them, and bring your parents. It's not the most fun you'll ever have, but the more help you get in this process, the better off you are.

ACE YOUR SCHOLARSHIP APPLICATIONS

You should apply for as many scholarships as humanly possible if you're serious about getting through college without a load of debt. Chances are you will have to take out some loans, but the more scholarships you have the less debt will weigh you down after you graduate. Scholarships are the best kind of financial aid you can get because you don't need to pay them back.

More than one billion dollars is given out in the form of scholarships each year to undergraduate students. That's a lot of money. You can earn a scholarship for all sorts of things—if you do well in school, write a certain essay, play a certain sport, speak a certain language, come from a certain racial or ethnic background, have a family member in the armed forces, plan to go into a certain field after college, or possess any number of other qualifications. Each year, many foundations and corporations award thousands of dollars in scholarship money that could be yours.

> *"I applied for LOTS of scholarships. The problem was, I applied for the general ones, the ones that are for "high school seniors and juniors" and "women under 35 with leadership potential." Everyone has something unique about him or her, be it an interest in community service, religion, sports, ethnicity, or another characteristic. Look it up—there is probably a scholarship for it!"*

There are many online resources and books where you can search for scholarships. Our favorite—and the most popular—is **www.FastWeb.com**. You can search based on your profile and find scholarships best suited for you.

The local businesses and organizations in your town will also give out many types of scholarships. Talk to your guidance counselor about where you can find applications for these scholarships and go after them.

Go after any scholarship for which you even remotely qualify, regardless of how small the amount. Every little bit helps, and often, there's less competition for smaller scholarships.

Remember that you have to report every scholarship that you receive to the colleges and universities where you apply and to the school that you decide to attend. They will likely lower the amount of your loans as a result, and the fewer loans you have, the better off you are.

"All throughout my senior year of high school, I applied for countless scholarships. I wrote essays about why I wanted to go to college, who my biggest role model was, what my Italian-American heritage has meant to me, and even why I thought Burger King symbolized the American Dream. I wrote my name, address, and social security number so many times, I thought I'd scream. In the end, I didn't even get close to half the number of scholarships I'd applied for. But, because I'd applied for so many, I got enough money that I haven't had to take out any loans so far to afford my education. I'm definitely grateful for that, and I realize now

that all that hassle and work back then was certainly worth it."

**Junior,
Cornell University**

☞ ACE YOUR SCHOLARSHIP ESSAY

We won't give you detailed advice on this topic—many great books already do—but here are a few general suggestions from our own experiences:

- Make sure that each essay is customized to the particular scholarship and organization where you're sending it. General essays don't work and they're easy to spot.

- Answer the question. Most scholarship essays will ask that you write on a particular topic or about a particular event. Stick to the instructions.

- Get to know the organization sponsoring each scholarship—what it does and what its goals and missions are. Then tailor your essay to touch on those themes, and describe what role they play in your life. For example, if you're applying for a scholarship from a non-profit organization that supports literacy, talk about why literacy is important and what you've done and will continue to do to promote it. Every organization has an agenda—find out what it is and target your essay appropriately.

- Don't whine. Don't spend your essay talking about how poor you are, how college is too expensive, how you're desperate to find any money, and so on. If you talk about difficulties in your life or your parents' lives, make sure that it's in the context of what you've learned form them.

- Try to sound human. Whoever is reading tons of these scholarship applications needs to find something in your essay that sticks out, that sounds personable and that he or she reader can relate to. Be honest with what you write and with your writing.

- Proofread. You've heard this before, and for a good reason. And don't trust the spellchecker—it can't tell the difference between "their" and "there."

- Follow directions. If the application asks you to put your name and email address on your essay, do it. If there is a word limit, stick to it.

! A WARNING ABOUT SCHOLARSHIP SCAMS

There are many places out there that will let you search large databases of scholarships for those that meet your needs, but you have to be careful. Some of these are not legitimate, and many of them will take your money if you're not careful. You can ask your guidance counselor for suggestions, but if you want to go looking on your own, here a few warning signs that a scholarship or a scholarship search service may not be completely legitimate:

- You have to give credit card or bank account information.

- The application costs money.

- The mailing address is a residential address, rather than a place of business.

- The service guarantees results—no one can guarantee that you'll receive a particular scholarship.

Before you apply for any scholarship you haven't heard of:

- Check with the local Better Business Bureau to make sure there are no complaints filed against the party in question. (Their website is **www.bbb.com**.)

- If the scholarship comes from a national foundation, make sure the foundation exists.

- Check with your school and your guidance counselor to see if anyone has heard of this scholarship or organization.

NAVIGATE THE LOAN MAZE

"The most challenging part about financial aid was understanding what my dad was talking about with fixed rates and subsidized loans and the economics of loans—if I had known those words meant thousands of dollars back then, I would have read up a bit more on what I was getting myself into."

**Recent Grad,
University of Wisconsin - Madison**

Although no one likes the idea of graduating with a load of debt, two-thirds of undergraduate students take out some type of loan to help them pay for college and, on average, students graduate with about sixteen thousand dollars in debt. This sounds like a lot, and it is, but you should find some comfort in the fact that millions of students just like you have managed to pay back these loans.

There are three general types of loans, outlined below. You should become familiar with them and understand what forms—besides the FAFSA—you'll have to fill out to apply for them. (But as we mentioned, the FAFSA is your first and most important step in the financial aid application process.)

▶**Student Loans**

Student loans are either provided or guaranteed by the government and they're the best kind of loans to get because they have extremely low interest rates.

The two most popular student loans are the <u>Stafford Loan</u> and the <u>Perkins Loan</u>.

The Stafford Loan can either be subsidized—the government pays the interest while you're in school—or unsubsidized—you're responsible for the interest, although you can usually defer actually paying it until you graduate. You have to qualify for financial aid in order to receive a subsidized Stafford Loan. As of 2002, the most you could borrow with a Stafford Loan is $2,625 during your freshman year, $3,500 during your sophomore year, and $5,500 for each additional year. Many students choose both the subsidized and unsubsidized loans to get the maximum amount.

Students who demonstrate exceptional financial need receive the Perkins Loan. Your college or university will actually administer this loan, but the funds are provided by the government. This is the best kind of loan that you can get—it's completely subsidized, and the government pays the interest while you're at school and for a nine-month grace period after you graduate. In 2002, you could borrow up to $3,000 per year in Perkins Loans, and you were limited to a total of $15,000.

"Now that I have finished college I can look back and see what I could have done differently. First of all, I would not have taken so many types of loans. Basically, I took whatever they would give me in loans that did not have interest accruing during school. This was a good strategy, but now I have four separate payments to make each month."

Recent Grad,
University of Wisconsin – Oshkosh

Whatever Stafford or Perkins loans you get, the money will go directly to the school each semester. You won't be getting a big fat check from the government or a private organization that's lending you money through the Perkins or Stafford program. In contrast, when you get a scholarship, you'll most likely be receiving a check from the organization sponsoring it—unless it's directly from your college, in which case the scholarship money may be dispersed directly to the bursar's office.

▶ Parent Loan for Undergraduate Students (PLUS)

Your parents can take out the PLUS loan to help pay for your education. They can borrow as much as they need to supplement the financial aid package that you receive, but they can't borrow more than that. This loan is the responsibility of your parents whereas the Stafford and Perkins loans are your responsibility to pay back.

▶ Private Loans

If your family does not receive enough financial aid in the form of Stafford, Perkins, PLUS loans, scholarships, and work-study, your parents might have to apply for additional loans from private lenders. There are many sources for this, but the terms are not as great as those that are provided or supported by the government.

DON'T MISS DEADLINES

Can you imagine anything worse than going through all the work of writing essays and filling out applications only to miss a deadline? Everything has a deadline, from the FAFSA to individual scholarship applications. To keep them all straight, write them down on your calendar or in your organizer that you regularly use.

And here's a little cheat technique that we've found works really well—if an application is due on March 1st, mark it down as due on February 15th so that you remember to send it out and get it there before the deadline. Every time you learn about a new scholarship that you plan to apply for, mark the due date in your calendar. Make sure that you know whether the due date is when your application must be post-marked or actually received. And never, ever, ever wait until the day before the deadline to submit your application—you never know what might happen to it in the postal service maze.

Deadlines also change from year to year, so don't use last year's due dates thinking they are the same as this year's.

LOOK UNDER EVERY ROCK

There are so many places to find money for college, and you should make sure you consider them all. Big or small, local or national, you should check into every resource. The billions of dollars given out in financial aid each year can help you pay for college, but they won't come looking for you.

Look everywhere. For example, your parents' employers might offer tuition benefits. The local business owners' association may have a scholarship for students planning to study business. The armed forces offer several options for students, including the Reserve Officer Training Corps (ROTC) program, which pays for tuition, fees, and books, and gives you a monthly allowance in exchange for a service commitment. There are tons of essay contests that are based on a certain topic or a book—even if the particular topic is not one you know a lot about, do some research, read the book, and write the essay.

A great place to visit to check into the many sources of aid for college is **www.FinAid.com**. It has clear explanations of every potential source, as well as links to scholarship search engines, specific programs, and government offices.

> *"I never thought that the local fireman's union would offer a $1,000 scholarship to a graduating senior in our high school...until I got it. I wish I'd checked out more resources rather than just focusing on national scholarships."*
>
> **Recent Grad,**
> **Wesleyan University**

DON'T RELY ON YOUR PARENTS

> *"Don't necessarily depend on your parents to do everything for you. I had a friend who got no aid last semester because he thought his dad had filled out all the papers, but his dad had completely forgotten, so he was in a bit of a bind."*
>
> **Sophomore,**
> **SUNY - Albany**

Don't assume that your parents will take care of all of the financial aid forms while you concentrate on filling out the actual college applications. If your parents tell you they will handle it, great, but don't assume that they will without talking to them about it. And even if your parents take on the burden to fill out forms like the FAFSA, looking for and filling out scholarship applications is your responsibility.

THE MORE, THE MERRIER

by
Christopher Wipf
Recent Grad, Dartmouth College

Financial aid offices have to brush off complaints every day from applicants who feel that they've been wronged. But if you can send over a copy of a more generous offer from somewhere else, that's quite a bit harder to ignore. My school decided to award me an additional $10,000 per year after seeing what other schools had committed. This made the time and toil of filling out a few extra applications very well spent!

Don't be afraid to lean on your parents. Have them call the school and explain why they don't have money to give you. For example, if your parents sell an investment off which they are going to live, and they thus have an unusually large amount of savings, have them explain the situation to your school.

Never let up on the financial aid department. Make phone calls, write letters, and speak with them in person. The more they know your name and your story, the more they will eventually tire of you and find some aid for you. If they tell you their hands are tied, seek higher help. Ask to talk to bosses of bosses. Persistence will pay off, and someone will eventually be able to help you come up with some money. The first offer they come up with may include loans, but try to hold out for the free money. All schools have special scholarship funds hidden away for special circumstances. Talk to the dean of your school—chances are, he or she has additional funds to help you.

Above all, try to remain professional. Money can become an emotional subject, especially if you find yourself up against a wall. In your letters, phone conversations, and in personal interviews, remain calm and continually state your troubles. Each person has unique circumstances, and the school will be willing to work with you.

☞ EARLY DECISION AND FINANCIAL AID

If you're thinking of applying Early Decision to a particular college, make sure that you understand the implications it has for financial aid. While you'll know if you're accepted by early winter, you won't receive your financial aid award until the spring, most likely in March or April, when admission letters for regular admission are sent out. <u>This means that you'll have to accept your offer of admission to your Early Decision school before you know what your financial aid award will be.</u>

This is very important. If you do get into your Early Decision school and accept the offer of admission, you're stuck with whatever financial aid package the school provides to you. Most colleges and universities use what's called Need-Blind Admission— meaning that they don't take your financial need into account when deciding whether to give you an offer. In many cases, schools will give you enough financial aid to make up the difference between your family's expected contribution and the cost of attending that particular school, but there are many exceptions. What the government and the school might estimate as your family's ability to pay may not always agree with your own assessment.

Don't rule out Early Decision just on this basis, but do think about it seriously. What you should definitely do is make sure that you're pretty certain that your Early Decision school is your number one choice.

15

make your
final decision

At last, the time has come for you to make your final decision about where to go to college. The first thing you should do is take a really, really deep breath—we've been there and we know just how exhausting and stressful this whole process has been. You got into college, and even if it's not your first choice, you should be psyched and take some time to enjoy this achievement. (You can start stressing about dealing with your roommate in a few months.)

It might be tempting to get this all over with and accept the first offer of admission that comes your way, but take some time to evaluate your options, if you have more than one. Go back to your ideal college profile, re-visit the schools if you have to, take financial aid into account, and make your choice. Then it's really time for a celebration!

DON'T RUSH
▼
EVALUATE YOUR OFFERS
▼
DEAL WITH BEING ON THE WAIT LIST
▼
DON'T DWELL ON REJECTION
▼
ACCEPT AN OFFER

DON'T RUSH

You receive your first fat envelope. Awesome. It's from your first choice. Even better. You want to accept immediately. Don't.

Even if it was your top choice when you applied, your priorities might have changed. Wait until you receive responses from all of the schools where you applied before making any decision and give yourself some time to think about your choices. Usually you'll have at least a few weeks to make up your mind.

EVALUATE YOUR OFFERS

If you have more than one acceptance offer—congratulations!—it might be challenging to decide which one to choose. All of these schools had something that appealed to you when you applied and now you have to eliminate all but one.

Go over your ideal college profile and any notes you might have made during your research and see how the schools measure up. Your priorities might have shifted during this time and what was critical when you applied may not be so important now.

"In the end it came down to Penn State and Bryn Mawr. I looked at the instructors they have, how many full-time, how many part-time, how many associate—Penn had 25 full-time professors and about 25 associates. I looked at their profiles and their areas of concentration. I made a grid with the different courses they offered—Penn had 71

courses, Bryn Mawr had 25. I looked at all of these things together before making my decision."

Sophomore,
Penn State University

If for some reason you haven't visited a school that has accepted you and you're considering going there, we strongly recommend that you figure out a way to go. A visit can make all the difference, either way.

For many of us financial aid plays a role. If a school you really like gave you much more aid than others, then your choice is probably clear. If your number one choice accepted you but didn't give you enough aid, don't be shy—call them up to ask for more money. This is not uncommon and you shouldn't feel strange about doing it. Tell them that you very much want to attend the school but you can't afford to do it without more aid. If you have a more generous offer from somewhere else, mention it and fax over the financial aid award letter—it can make a huge difference in making your case. Be persistent.

It might be that your first choice doesn't fork over more money and you have to consider whether you and your family can or want to take out additional loans. This is a very personal decision and our only advice is to think about it for a while and make sure that you want to go to this school for all the right reasons.

Finally, get some advice. Talk to your guidance counselor and your parents and see what they think about where you should go. It's your decision, but you might hear something that helps you make your selection.

WE TALK WITH...

Amy Rodgers
Recent Grad, Columbia University

How many schools did you apply to and at how many were you accepted?

I applied to Columbia and Rutgers and then had to make the decision about which one to attend.

How did you go about deciding between the two?

I went to a visiting day at each school. I got to meet some of the deans and there were a couple of students there who were currently attending and you could ask them questions. I got to talk to people who worked in the areas that I was interested in.

What did you learn or gain from talking to people there?

I really liked the people in the administration to whom I spoke. I talked to students and they had good things to say. The worst thing they had to say about Columbia was that it was kind of pricey. But they felt their experience had been top quality.

What else did you do to help you decide?

I sat in on classes because I wanted to get an idea of what kind of discussions students were having with their professors. The class I sat in on at Columbia was not super-formal or hierarchical—that really appealed to me.

After weighing up the pros and cons, how did you decide?

This sounds really weird, but ultimately, I went with my gut.

DEAL WITH BEING ON THE WAIT LIST

Being on a wait list is frustrating. And there's just no way to predict what will happen. The number of people accepted from wait lists varies considerably from school to school and from year to year. It's not a comfortable place to be, but look on the positive side—you could still get in.

Just because you're on the wait list at one school, it doesn't mean that you should wait to make a decision about where to go. If you've been accepted at other schools, think about them, and if one is a great match then go ahead and accept the offer. Many schools don't know if there will be space until after May 1st—the deadline for letting colleges know your decision—and you don't want to miss out on a really great school by hanging out in wait-list limbo.

It's all too easy to start thinking that a particular school is better because it wait-listed you. It's not. Just because you're on the wait list does not mean that the school is higher quality or more competitive. Schools put students on wait lists for many reasons and you shouldn't try to guess what yours was.

If you really believe that the college that wait-listed you is your best match, you can try to take some action to encourage your acceptance. Send a polite letter to the admissions office and tell them that this is your number one choice and that you strongly want to attend. Schools worry about making offers to students who don't accept them and your indication of interest might get you off the wait list. You can also let the school know if anything has happened since you applied that you think might improve your chances. If your most recent grades are excellent or if you received some sort of an award or honor, let the school know.

Talk to your guidance counselor about these options before you take any action. She or he might be able to provide you with some insight into how to word your letter or what things you're better off not sending to the school.

DON'T DWELL ON REJECTION

It's nearly impossible not to take rejection personally. You've invested a lot of time and energy into the admissions process, and no matter what anyone says, rejection just doesn't feel good. Acknowledge that you're disappointed, hurt, or angry, but try not to dwell on it. You're not stupid or incompetent because you got rejected, and perhaps this is a blessing in disguise to keep you from going to a school where you'd be miserable.

"To some extent this is all a game of chance. Colleges are always going to have many more qualified applicants than they can accept. Say you wanted to go to Columbia and you didn't get in, but you did get into Duke. Inevitably there's going to be somebody who really wanted to get into Duke and didn't, but got into Columbia. That always happens, and you have to have a certain amount of acceptance about that. There are so many incredible schools out there, and we tend to hear about five or six or them, when in reality there are really hundreds of great universities where you could be really happy."

**Recent Grad,
Columbia University**

ACCEPT AN OFFER

> *"Getting accepted to the school where I really felt that I belonged was an amazing outcome of all the work I'd done in high school. I felt like I'd achieved something I'd really worked for."*

Junior,
Vassar College

In all the excitement mixed with exhaustion, don't forget to accept an offer from your school of choice. You have until May 1st if you applied under regular admission, and you need to notify the school prior to that deadline. You'll likely have to send in a deposit and a roommate questionnaire, although requirements vary by school.

If you've been accepted at more than one school, make sure that you also notify the schools you will not be attending. Remember, there's a student out there on a wait list who's just dying to get that spot.

And then finally: EXHALE!

IF AT FIRST YOU DON'T SUCCEED

by
Holly Popowski
Senior, New York University

Ahhh, the college application process. One of the most nerve-racking experiences you'll ever know. My personal experience was rather unique. My senior year turned out to be a very hectic time, and I never really had the time to visit any colleges or get organized with the applications. My grades were decent, but not great, I had some good letters of recommendation, but I didn't have what I felt would be a strong enough application to get into any really good schools. Instead, I only applied to one school, a mid-tier public school, and I spent my first year there trying to figure out how to escape.

I worked really hard, got on the Dean's list, joined five clubs, became editor of the newspaper, took on an internship, and made friends with a few of my professors. I finally felt prepared to apply to some better schools, hoping they would want me as a transfer student. I ended up getting into New York University—a great school for a philosophy major. I never would've gotten in if it weren't for the fact that I'd proven myself at my first college.

If I could offer you one piece of advice it would be this: If you don't get into the school you want, go to your safety school, do really well, work really hard, and then re-apply to your top choice. It will show the school that you're serious about getting an education at their institution and that you can do well in a university setting.

16

the
daily grind

Regardless of your grades and scores, how organized you are with your applications, or how you feel about going to college in the first place, there are going to be times when you feel frustrated and overwhelmed during the college application process. And that's completely normal because it is overwhelming! Here are a few things to keep in mind as you deal with the daily grind of the college application process:

►CREATE A ROUTINE

One of the biggest challenges in the college application process is that you have to work consistently—whether it's researching schools or writing your essays—for a pretty long period of time. You're going to go nuts unless you organize your time in some way that makes it manageable on a day-to-day basis.

We found that one of the best ways to stay on track is to maintain a regular schedule. Get used to working on some part of your college search or your applications for a few hours each day, several days a week. Set daily and weekly objectives and try to stick to them as much as you can. You should also schedule in a few college-free days here and there to give yourself and your mind a break.

▶KEEP AN OPEN MIND

If you know what you want out of your ideal college and your education, you're off to a great start. Just keep in mind that a school with all of your desired qualities may not exist. To keep yourself from going crazy looking for that one perfect college, try to be flexible and recognize that you'll have to compromise on some qualities to get those that are most important to you.

Keeping an open mind is also important because as you go through this process you'll learn a great deal about yourself and what you thought you wanted in a college might change quite a bit. Don't feel like change is bad or that you have to stick to your initial criteria.

▶GET HELP WHEN YOU NEED IT

No matter how bright, organized, or focused you may be, you're doing something you've never done before, so you're going to need help and guidance to get through it. Even if you're not someone who likes to ask for help, this isn't the best time to go it alone. Your friends, parents, counselors, and advisors can be a great support network and can often help you with specific issues as well, such as looking for scholarships or commenting on your essays.

▶REMEMBER THAT IT'S YOUR DECISION

You're going to get a lot of advice during this time—whether you ask for it or not. Sometimes advice-givers will raise useful points or come up with ideas that hadn't occurred to you. At other times they may give you advice that is not relevant or helpful.

Be open to suggestions and input and don't try to get through this difficult process all on your own. But remember that at the end of the day, where you apply to college and what your essay is about are your decisions and you have to feel comfortable with them.

▶MAINTAIN SOME PERSPECTIVE

This is sometimes hard to do, but try not to think of where you go to college and whether you get accepted at your number one choice school as a life or death decision. Your college education is tremendously important and it will have an impact on your future, but remember that you can get a good education wherever you go, as long as you're willing to work for it.

You're not a failure if you don't get into your top choice school. It happens to thousands of the brightest and most ambitious students every year and it has nothing to do with you being stupid or incompetent. The college admissions process is complicated, filled with subjective decisions and many factors over which you have no control.

Be proud of where you get accepted and focus on how you'll make your college years really great.

17

helpful
resources

Here are a few of our favorite resources—listed in no particular order—that will help you in your college search and with acing your college apps.

☞ BOOKS

The Best 331 Colleges, by Edward Custard. Princeton Review. Published annually.

Tens of thousands of college students were asked to tell the whole truth about their colleges. Their answers are in this book. As well as revealing insider information, it also provides practical information like campus addresses, online addresses, phone numbers, deadlines, as well as statistics on admission selectivity, student population, financial aid, and more.

The Fiske Guide to Colleges, by Edward B. Fiske. Sourcebooks, Inc. Published annually.

Thousands of students and administrators are surveyed for this guide, which has been in publication for more than twenty years. It covers more than 300 colleges and universities, describing such things as setting, academic and social tone, professor/student interaction, as well as scholarship opportunities.

Greenes' Guide to Educational Planning: The Public Ivies, by Howard Greene and Mathew Greene. Cliff Street Books, 2001.

If you're looking for a school with a low price tag, this book will tell you how to receive a top-notch education for a fraction of what you'd pay at a private school. Thirty of the best public colleges and universities are profiled.

Barron's Best Buys in College Education, by Lucia Solorzano. Barron's Educational Series, 6th Edition, 2000.

This book aims to help you find a bargain without compromising on quality. There are "Quick Lists" to help you target schools by particular characteristics, such as size, price, etc. This is followed by profiles of nearly 300 colleges, both private and public, listed alphabetically.

Colleges that Change Lives, by Lauren Pope. Penguin Books, 2000.

Written by a College Bureau Placement Director, this book profiles forty colleges noted for developing student potential. The book evaluates colleges in terms of both program offerings and tone, and includes interviews with undergraduates, deans, and professors.

Cool Colleges for the Hyper-Intelligent, Self-Directed, Late Blooming, and Just Plain Different, by Donald Asher. Ten Speed Press, 2000.

This book provides the inside scoop on what schools are like for the students who go there. There are lots of fun and interesting facts about various colleges, application hints, and tips for life while at college.

Visiting College Campuses, by Janet Spencer and Sandra Maleson. Princeton Review Publishing, 1998.

Everything you need to help you plan your college visits is in this book. It profiles 249 of the most-visited campuses, providing information on how to get there by any mode of transportation, where to stay, the best and worst times of year to visit, and the dates and times that campus tours are available. A mileage chart of distances between campuses and academic calendars for each school are just some of the other useful inclusions.

10 Real SATs, by The College Board. College Board, 2003.

This book is great for practicing for the SAT. As the title suggests, it contains ten real SAT I tests from past years. You can't get any better practice than this.

100 Successful College Application Essays, by the Harvard Independent. New American Library Trade, 2nd Edition, 2002.

Generally we would say that you should try to avoid reading too many essays by other people and take your own unique approach. However, if you're stuck and need some inspiration, try reading the essays in this book. It includes helpful commentary as well.

On Writing the College Application Essay, by Harry Bauld. Barnes & Noble, 1987.

Written by a former Ivy League admissions officer, this book is a great help and inspiration. Check it out.

 **WEBSITES**

www.campustours.com

Can't make it to all the colleges you're considering? Go there virtually instead. This site, organized by state, offers virtual tours of numerous universities. While it's always better to visit colleges in person, this can be a good starting point to help you narrow down your choices.

www.wiredscholar.com

This is a great all-around website for college-bound students. It covers everything from preparing and selecting to applying and paying. It has some really great checklists that you can print out and use to help you get ready for school interviews and visits, and make sure that you're up to speed on your application and financial-aid paperwork.

www.collegeboard.com

This site is filled with information about all aspects of the college admissions process. It also covers the different financing options available for college students. It has a useful tool to help you compare financial aid awards and there's another tool you can use to do quick, side-by-side comparisons of two or three colleges.

www.nacac.com

Use this site, of the National Association for College Admission Counseling, to locate college fairs in your area.

www.finaid.com

This website has tons of information about financial aid. It's presented clearly and can be a great help as you navigate this maze.

www.fafsa.ed.gov

This site is an invaluable resource for students seeking financial aid. Here you can determine if you're eligible for aid, get applicable forms and documents, fill out worksheets, check the status of your submitted forms, and actually fill out forms and submit them online.

www.commonapp.org

This website, as the address suggests, is home to the Common Application. It lists all the schools that use the Common Application, as well as which schools require supplements. You can download the common application, as well as many of the colleges' supplements.

www.princetonreview.com

There's not much on this website that you can't do. Whether you want information on a particular school, advice about applications, help with test prep (you can even search for a course or tutor in your area), free practice tests, school match (you fill out a profile and they match you with a right school), help searching for a scholarship, information on paying for school, or if you're ready to apply and want to download applications—it's all available here.

www.xap.com

On this site you can apply to schools, practice your SATs, explore a career path, look up information on colleges, figure out financial aid options, and much more.

www.studentshelpingstudents.com

We can't miss an opportunity to plug this website filled with student-written articles on everything from finding scholarships to applying to college, and much more.

18

the
final word

Applying to college is many things—stressful, competitive, time consuming, sleep depriving—but it's definitely not easy. It's our hope that the advice in this book helps you both get things done better and preserve your sanity as you go through this process. Remember that though it may seem tough at times, the application process is really the beginning of a great time in your life: COLLEGE!

Whatever the outcome, we found that we all felt a sense of accomplishment at the end of it all and hope that you will, too. Do your best and remember that wherever you go, you can make your college experience as great and productive as you wish.

Congrats on getting through it and good luck!

- Siobhan, Megan & Albert